Biting Silence

C. L. Methvin

Sinister Stoat Press

Biting Silence
C.L. Methvin

ISBN-13: 978-1-948712-22-4

Artwork for full cover by Florian-Ayala Fauna (she/her)
www.Florian-93.com
sinewaves23@gmail.com
Cover title: By the Throat
Back cover Polaroids: untitled

© 2022 C.L. Methvin

Sinister Stoat Press
an Imprint of Weasel Press
Lansing, MI
https://www.weaselpress.com/sinisterstoatpress

ALL RIGHTS RESERVED. This book contains material protected under International and Federal Copyright Laws and Treaties. Any unauthorized reprint or use of this material is prohibited. No part of this book, or use of characters in this book, may be reproduced or transmitted in any form or by any means, electronic or mechanical, including photocopying, recording, or by any information storage and retrieval system without express written permission from the author / publisher.

Author's Note:

Burden of Representation:
    When individuals of a marginalized group and/or their actions are viewed as representing the entirety of said group.

As a queer author writing queer characters, I am aware of the burden of representation. I am similarly refusing it. Many of my characters are queer. Many are similarly awful. They represent themselves and only themselves. If you ascribe the actions of one queer individual to all of them, this book is not for you.

For those that need them, content warnings can be found on the bottom of the following page. For those to whom content warnings may be considered spoilers, feel free to skip over it.

Content Warnings:
Murder, self-harm, suicide, animal violence, kink violence, alcohol/drugs, dissociative/depressive descriptors

Biting silence

What are you doing?
What am I doing?
The evening settled over the building in a cold silence. The sun was in the early stages of setting and gifted the world with a soft orange glow. It was mid-winter and the weather reflected as much—frost teased leaves, wind chilled to the core, and nights were long and unforgivingly bitter. Aften knew as much, and as he lay on the couch of his shared apartment, he expected this night to be more of the same. Much as the night, he too was bitter.

Hey man, you there?
We still on for later this week?
Party tonight. Last minute, you coming?

Aften stared at his phone, waiting not for someone to contact him (because people had) but to feel confident enough to respond. Though the time flew by—hour to hours to more—he fingered the screen and prodded at nothings while every forty-five minutes or so another text came through that made him want to cry. Each message was friendly and all welcoming and Aften had no idea how to respond to them. Only recently had he branched out and began actively associating with people—friends? —that took him places: parties, bars, houses of people he had never met; it was all so extravagant and delightful though equally overwhelming. "I'm anxious," he would say unironically, but taper with a laugh (this laugh made it easier to say) —an honest self-deprecation that people ignored: "Well come out anyway!"

There was an anxiety within him that made compliments tough. Not in regard to content, for the flattery could be mundane, sexual, or anything in-between, but in his ability to receive it without doubt.

Lying on his side, depressing into the cushions of his futon, a hyperawareness overtook him: internal judgement made him far too aware of his sallow eyes, his messy black hair. A tired gaze traveled along his arm—he wasn't in bad shape, though neither notable—until he eventually inspected his torso: flat, collar bones protruding, very thin, pale build but with no muscle to complement it.

Further, he inspected himself. The more he did, the more he wished he hadn't.

Aften pulled himself from the couch and a headache swirled inside him. He readjusted his boxer-briefs (for "why wear clothes if you don't have plans?" (This he had repeated for the last four days)) before stumbling into the kitchen. His breakfast had cooled in the coffee pot—Dark Roast he'd forgotten about. A glance again at his phone: it was six p.m.

Reaching into the sink, he grabbed a mug and shook it dry before pouring the coffee (again, shaking the pot first) into his cup. Breakfast had become dinner.

There was a leftover take-out box pushed against the microwave. Looking at it, his stomach growled with a hollow memory of hunger: he couldn't remember eating anything after it. The receipt taped to the side was dated for two days earlier.

The coffee tasted like shit. Aften dragged his tongue across his upper teeth and scoffed before dumping the foam-topped brown down the drain.

I'm going to kill myself.

Matthew's bed was a goddamn mess as Heather rolled out of it. A stretch and a yawn followed before she brushed her hair aside and smiled: she'd dyed her hair this light purple and silver combination, like a softer thistle flower.

"We slept way too late." She tugged a shirt over her head. Looking down, she realized it was Matthew's shirt.

Matthew smiled in return. He let out a groan as he rolled to fill Heather's spot. His skin was a russet color, if not a shade darker, his eyes brown; his hair was in the early budding stages on the path to dreadlocks—something he was both excited for and impatient in its wait. Intermittent beams of light permitted themselves to slice the two of them into bars. "We didn't do much sleeping."

They both laughed. Matthew's hand fumbled around atop his nightstand until it wrapped around the neck of a third-full vodka bottle. He took a quick swig and grunted, checking the clock beside him: it was a little after six.

"Shit, Heather." He was legitimately surprised. "Six in the evening?" He uprooted quickly and peeked between the blinds at the setting sun.

"Told you we slept too late."

He hastily grabbed a pair of jeans and shirt from his floor—he'd looked for a belt though quickly gave up—and squinted at his phone in the dimly-lit afternoon.

Somewhere on the floor they both heard Matthew's cat roll around. "Biscuit, c'mere." Heather bent down and stroked the cat. He was comfortably embedded in a pile of laundry. Cat hair drifted in the air and rested in haphazard patterns in the threads of their clothing.

The room smelled musty and was arguably sweatier than the rest of the house—a fact Matthew learned upon opening the bedroom door to a house more acclimated to the brisk December about them. "When is the party exactly?"

"Sara said it was at her place at...seven? I think." Heather continued scratching Biscuit under the chin. Biscuit was deep gray save his green eyes. He melded with the fabric shadows almost organically. The cat purred. "Seven or eight, yeah?"

"Should we ask Aften if he wants to come?"

"I would," Heather answered. "I'd like for him to. Plus, I'd feel bad if we just left him to go see people that are also his friends."

"But Ethan will also be there. He lives with Sara, after all." Matthew reminded her.

Heather pondered that point. Aften and Ethan had a…tumultuous relationship after the two stopped dating. All seemed well between them until Ethan broke Aften's wrist, at which point, accompanied by a great deal of screaming, their relationship came to an end.

"Well," She began to tease, "Maybe after a few drinks tonight, you two can fuck to make up for it when we get home."

Matthew would not be opposed. He and Aften had (on multiple occasions) had sex with the other. And while Heather knew this, she still enjoyed vicariously resurfacing the memory. Matthew obliged. "That's not a bad suggestion." If Heather was to try and fluster him, he refused to let her succeed.

Heather offered a sideways smile. She found a bottle of hard cider half-finished resting against the bedframe and indulged herself. It was flat but alcoholic—that's all she was really looking for.

The tip of the knife made a light *shiing!* sound as Aften scraped it along the countertop. His bare feet dragged in the shag carpet, his head was low; the bathroom door was welcoming and the lights above the mirror—two lit, three dark—bathed him in septic yellow. In his reflection he saw the door behind him shut, the knob locked—though he didn't remember doing so; he'd been too occupied with the silver in his grip.

There was a low, incandescent hum prickling within him as he stared at his arm. Still as thin as it was twenty minutes ago, except now the blue beneath it was more prominent—these tiny, canopied rivers flowing beneath him. Gently, Aften pressed the blade to his left wrist—it was cold, but that came as no surprise. He grew more aware of his breathing: hefty, strained breaths that rose against the knife with each pulse of his nervous forearm.

He tossed the knife into the sink. It danced in reply as he subsequently pushed his hands to the pseudo-granite and hissed "God...God..." between watered teeth. Aften wiped the drool from his lower lip and cleared the gathering tears from his eyes. "Fuck...God." It was harder than he had anticipated. It was supposed to be simple, clean; it was supposed to be an easy way to close his eyes and never open them, to drag this knife, to fall to the ground; to get dizzy and topple over, like getting high, or drunk, and just kind of slowly drifting away, only this time without a hangover.

Aften shook his head—everything was a little blurry, but in its own way that made things easier. He reached into the sink and picked up the knife again, flipped it appropriately in his hand, and once more drew it to his arm.

And, again, he could not bring himself to do it.

He glared at himself in the mirror, this time angry: "Do it, do it you little bitch." It was harder to feel this time—he couldn't explain why. Looking at his reflection—looking at his reflection, instead of himself—his *actual* self—made it easier. His chest rose, so did his head—he found himself staring down the bridge of his nose to see what he was doing. His breathing grew faster and faster as internally he continued to berate his sick cowardice until, eventually, with an unfamiliar swiftness and resolution he threw his head to the side and dragged the metal across his trembling arm.

His body rang with a grating, inward whisper.

The world rang silent for the briefest of moments.

Sara was applying eyeliner in the mirror of her vanity while, behind her, somewhat loudly, Ethan was fucking Sara's girlfriend. She dragged the pencil across her lower lid, unsure totally if it was even (for the light was dimmed, her mirror only half-lit rightwards by a teal slag-glass lamp (Ethan and Jessíka wanted the room dark)). It was annoying.

Ethan's grunts were boring and immemorable; Jessíka afforded him too much credit—she lay on her back, legs wrapped around his hips as they and the bed moaned. Ethan's hair was a blonde, swaying net, coming to stop right above his reddened shoulders. Sara couldn't fathom how someone had managed to become sunburnt in winter, yet found it expectable that if anyone could it would be Ethan. Sara perked up however upon redirecting her gaze to Jessíka. Even sweating she was gorgeous—teeth only slightly lighter than almonds, pink lips, sandy skin—Sara was enamored. Watching her writhe and contort against sheets, she mused excitedly at the thought of recreating the scene with her tongue. She turned back to her vanity.

There was a party later. Sara should know—she was hosting it. Very little was ready in terms of presentation: she hadn't been downstairs in well over twelve hours, and she doubted the competence of her roommates to prepare the house. Regarding food and drink she was well-stocked—or, rather, would be: it was a "bring-your-own" sort of thing. She had finished her eyeliner to the best of her patience and instead decided to play with her lips. Red was cliché; purple was too much for today; teal was out of the question; she settled for black. She typically settled for black.

There was a knock.

Sara stopped applying her lipstick. "Yeah?" The soft squeaking of the bed and the less-soft squeaking of Jessíka overshadowed the creak of the door as Mercer let himself in. He had facial hair that had grown in soft patches over red cheeks (both of which were barely visible in the dim of the room). He pushed his hair out of his face, which was in the frustrating stage of being neither quite long enough nor short enough for Mercer to decide whether or not he wished to cut it.

Mercer briefly registered the two tangled bodies before redirecting his attention to Sara. "Did you eat my leftovers?" His voice betrayed him by softly breaking as he spoke.

"I don't remember the last time I was even in the kitchen."

"That didn't answer my question."

Sara turned, visibly frustrated. "No, I did not." She did not say it, but had no doubt it had been Ethan.

Mercer turned towards the bed. "Did one of you?"

Ethan paused, breathing heavy. He had one hand flat against the bed, the other holding Jessíka's foot over his shoulder. "Was it—was it Italian or some shit?" Ethan asked. Jessíka's exaggerated moans settled as the sex was interrupted by a fucking dinner discussion.

"Yes."

"Yeah man, that was me." Ethan resumed at a slow pace. Sara was in no way surprised. Jessíka seemed noticably less interested in sex following this interuption.

Mercer looked to Sara and mouthed, "What the *fuck*?" Sara did not have time for this. She stood from her mirror and instead sauntered to the bed. Pressing her knees into the knotted comforter, she laid against Ethan's back, one hand resting flat on his chest and the other reaching down to explore Jessíka's calf. While not immediate, Sara slowly felt his thrusting come to a halt. He was softly panting. His tank was doused in sweat and the stitching of the collar stretched beyond repair. The lamp flickered briefly, and in its teal light Sara saw Jessíka's brown eyes glint like sunken gems.

"Go downstairs," Sara said to Ethan. "Clean up before the guests arrive."

Ethan groaned, but Jessíka reaffirmed Sara's orders by pushing him off of her. She slid back and rested against the headboard before yawning, "When are they getting here anyway?"

Mercer tossed Ethan a pair of boxers from the hamper next to him. "Any time between seven and eleven. We have a hard cut-off point around then; no one ever wants to leave if they come any later." No longer (as) frustrated by the subject of his stolen dinner, Mercer could appreciate the room. It was messier than his, but messy in such a way that evoked an envy for the love put into becoming so. Dumb little statues decorated dressers; the bed's headboard displayed a mix of stuffed animals, cups, and jewlery; inconsistently-framed photos were nailed to the walls. While a mess, it was one of comfort.

Sara sat down next to Jessíka and planted a gray kiss on her jaw. "Is Matt coming?" Jessíka asked. She drew her legs up and leaned her head on Sara's while Ethan pulled on a pair of track pants. They were slim, cute, and did well to compliment what little definition there was to Ethan's frame. Sara looked elsewhere. The walls were off-beige below the lamp's teal glow. There were square patches of lighter tints from where Jessíka had arranged and again rearranged picture frames. Had the property been a rental, such yellowed walls would be an inarguable problem when leases arose, but through the misfortune of death and the fortune of inheritance, the house had been left to Sara by her late grandmother to disrespect as she pleased. It was only now upon seeing the stained outlines that Sara realized the bedroom window had been open and letting light in beyond her deskside lamp, albeit dim. She shivered, as if only now aware of the cold.

"Yeah, texted Matt earlier," Ethan responded. He scraped under his nail and proceeded to light a cigarette. He continued to hold the flame beneath his hand for a few moments—he liked the warmth. Most of his fingertips were tinged gray with inattention. The fire alarms had been dissected of their batteries years ago. "Haven't heard from Aften." Ethan spoke through aggravated, pursed lips, "but Matt's coming, and he'll *probably* bring him along."

Jessíka averted her eyes. Ethan and Aften's problems were not hers and she—all of them, really—made the effort to keep it that way.

Ethan slid into his sneakers—no socks—and walked past Mercer in the doorframe, who promptly messed up Ethan's hair.

"Fuck off, dude.

"Much love to you too."

And in a weird way, it was out of love, of friendship, but none of them quite knew how to show it beyond bothering one another.

At first he didn't feel anything. Or at least, he didn't think he did. There was an adrenaline pulsing through his arms, his jawline—the only sensation that verified the cut was the trickling along his forearm, soon following the rivulets of his palm.

And then the pain finally surfaced.

He looked down with one eye tightly shut as a soundless gasp escaped his shuddering mouth. He fucking missed. He didn't know what he wanted to hit, but he knew he had missed it. Skin peeled back like a small chasm as his insides pushed out in waves, flowing along his arm in red that splattered the counter indiscriminately. The blade fell onto the plush mat beneath him—barely missing his right foot—as he staggered back a little before frantically thrusting his arm forward so that his blood collected in the sink. With his free hand he wrapped around his arm, watching the red trickle through the crevices and waterfall along his fingers.

"Fuck, fuck, shit." Aften hastily grabbed a washcloth and stumbled into the shower—part of the curtain ripped from its bearings as he slammed into the tile. The slightly wet, indented flooring transformed from clear to pink to crimson and back to pink while the showerhead burst forth cold water. He wrapped the fabric around his wrist and watched a rust-colored splotch devour the rugged cloth.

Lowering his head, the water rushed through his hair and the chill widened his eyes; his whole body shivered, though his attention was invested in tightening the force on his injury. Aften's arms quivered as he held them to his sides—he bent at the knees and curled inward while pressing his forehead to the laminate base. He grit his teeth, his quiet sobs lost to the indifferent water.

Aften pushed himself up ever-so-lightly, eyes staring half-focused at his chest: it was painted pink, a grotesque cavity along his sternum that the rushing cold forced into line. Yet…he found his tongue gently pressing against the roof of his mouth, worry replaced with intrigue, and as that warm redness washed down his torso, then his legs, there came an inexplicable stiffness between them. His fingers—for the first time, not trembling—traced along the base of his ribs before following the trickling water through the red. Carefully, delicately, exploring the thick warmness, his hand was soon wound within a soft and rhythmic grip.

Aften gasped.

Faster and tighter did the motions continue as his arched back rocked forward, backward, forward again. The icy downrush heightened the warmth of his breath rolling over his tongue, the warmth of his blood rolling down his cock, along his thighs—Aften gasped again and collapsed lightly against the freezing wall. Through dizzied eyes and with a light head he bit his lower lip as with one final, aching convulsion did he climax into a deep-red palm. He licked the back of his shivering hand and tasted the salt, the copper. Though the wound was exhausting itself, still it bled, yet Aften could not feel the pain through the euphoria with which it was replaced.

The cold disappeared alongside the strained pulsing, all feeling replaced with heavy-breathed elation. His cum slipped through his fingers and splashed below him, yet his attention was stolen by...something. The curtain shifted, and from the corner of his eyes, Aften could swear he saw something small and gray scuttle down the bathtub border.

He paused, scanned the room, and breathed an exhausted sigh before he had even begun. Ethan hated when Sara held parties. It always meant having to clean.

With a trash bag in one hand he scouted their living room, picking up cups, boxes, wrappers of various kinds; most were his and Mercer's but it didn't assuage his disdain for cleaning. His hand danced around their bookshelves, displacing dust and replacing novels. Mercer and Jessíka read regularly but seemed incapable of putting them back. He admired their erudition; he instead was skilled in arts—this was one of the few things he and Sara had in common. Both their works decorated the living room: Sara's paintings, and Ethan's fixtures. Above Mercer's lectern (which, at every opportunity, he would remind you is an antique) hung a scrap-metal owl, the tips of its wings lined with bulbs that cascaded against the walls. Ethan was most proud of that piece.

Others were scattered about, illuminating the walls, paintings, tapestries; very little of their wallspace was free of decoration, nearly all of it vintage, or "vintage," or some sort of dark art piece. The only one vaguely recognizable was a reprint of Goya; all others were collected from various antique stores or secondhand shops, and the house was generally in agreement that none held any authenticity. Even so, Ethan enjoyed the aesthetic save for the dying plants, but knew Mercer loved the look: "It's humbling, watching other things die. A somber reminder to appreciate yourself," or something to that effect. Intentionally letting plants die, however, bothered Jessíka, and by extension bothered Ethan.

The scent of patchouli and ash lingered in the stagnant air, to which Ethan contributed by lighting another cigarette. He paused after doing so, realizing he had no idea what he'd done with the one he had started in Sara's room, victim yet again to his own absentmindedness. The lapse of memory might have anyone rightfully concerned, but not Ethan—this seemed just as good a reason to justify another smoke. He propped his feet on the coffee table and sank into the itchy floral couch opposite their television, an important step in the cleaning process. The television had been left on for God knows how long, its subtle gray pouring onto the matted carpet below it.

"What are you watching?" Sara asked, descending the stairs.

"I'm not really sure."

Some sort of botanist show was playing in the background. "Mercer must have last been watching."

"Wasting electricity."

"He probably forgot."

"Doesn't make it less of a waste."

Ethan snubbed his cigarette in a dragon-shaped ashtray and stood, stretching. He didn't wish to argue. He did not care for Sara, Sara did not care for him, and to neither of them was such dislike a secret. "I better keep cleaning."

Sara didn't argue. "Why is it so cold?" she asked as though it were not mid-winter.

Ethan ignored the question. "Do you think Heather is coming? Did we invite her?"

"I'm pretty sure we did. I mean, we invited Matt; there's no way we'd only invite one of 'em."

"But you don't know?"

"Mercer did," Sara declared, though uncertain. She picked up Ethan's half-finished cigarette and relit it. She knew this was Ethan's way of asking if Aften were coming, and they both knew Aften would be. Ethan just wanted to be mad at something, and Sara refused to answer in a way that allowed it.

Ethan opted to fight anyway: "You all could have at least told me."

"And you could have *not* beaten Aften, but you did." Sara retorted with fire in her voice. "And now you have to deal with the fact that people won't help you avoid your own consequences."

"That's not—"

"Yes, yes, we all know—it's *complicated*," she cut him off. "You went too far, you broke his wrist or arm or whatever, but somehow you want to defend yourself."

She was right, Ethan could admit—he did want to defend himself, but she similarly did not pause to allow him to.

"—and so help me God just leave him alone tonight. I don't care what you have to say—just don't. Let everyone enjoy themselves tonight. The fucking end."

Ethan had so much more to say but none of the words would come out, none felt like they would satisfy. His eyes were wide, incredulous, but in that moment the nuance of his and Aften's past relationship was without explanation. *Just don't leave visible bruises.* Ethan had fucked that rule up royally.

A change of subject from Ethan: "You gonna help clean?"

The same frustration from Sara: "You gonna pay rent?"

Ethan bit his tongue. He'd graduated, but an arts degree challenged him. His three roommates had been more than patient as he was between jobs—no longer receiving scholarly refunds to sustain his living—so he decided it best not to argue further. He was begrudgingly resigned in his responsibility to clean until otherwise capable of contributing. "How's Jessíka been lately? I'm never sure how to ask her.'"

Sara shrugged. Her demeanor seemed to relax on the subject of her girlfriend. "She's doing better now, on antidepressants. Doing better."

Ethan didn't pry. Sara exhaled smoke and watched it dance with the dust in the air.

"What the fuck was that?" Heather asked, turning to the wall. Biscuit had since darted off.

Matthew was applying deodorant and stumbling, trying to slip his feet into laced shoes (it wasn't going well). "Aften must have tripped in the shower. He's...always kinda dizzy." Heather stared, raising an eyebrow at Matthew's unbothered preparation.

"...what?"

"Matt you are such an asshole."

"I'm not his babysitter—he can stand back up on his own."

Heather fell into the bed, arms outstretched and looked to Matthew before whispering, "*Asshooooole.*"

He followed suit, falling atop her—one hand on either side—and looked at her with an expression of fake pensiveness. The posters lining the walls looked down at them: bands and movies and other eventful trinkets. The ones closer to the floor bore the scars of Biscuit's interest, for the cat didn't care much for Matthew's memories. "Okay, fine—I will go check. But it will cost you one kiss."

"Hmm," Heather pondered. She looped a finger through one of his beltloops. "That's kind of steep. I will offer one half-kiss." Before Matthew could continue their negotiation, she reached up and planted her lips on his cheek. "There. Now, stop being a jerk and go check on your goddamn roommate."

He rolled his eyes and pushed himself up; his shirt was decorated with cat hair. Most of his clothes were.

Matthew gave up on his shoes and yawned through his doorway before, locking eyes with Heather, knocking on the door of their bathroom. Heather stuck out her tongue.

"Aften. Aften, you alright in there man?"

There was more stumbling and a muffled "*shit*."

Now Matthew's demeanor took on a more serious presentation as he knocked harder, which Heather noticed: she sat up, visibly confused. She mouthed, "he okay?" to which Matthew could only shrug. It was not unlike Aften to be clumsy, though the exclamation was a more immediate indication to Matthew that something was definitely wrong. A fumbling noise sounded and a heavy *stomp* (Aften probably slipped and caught himself, Matthew reasoned) as the lock of the door rattled. Aften cracked the door.

"Holy *shit* dude!" Now Matthew stumbled slightly, caught wholly off-guard by the sight.

Blood was smeared across Aften's face, below his nose, down his chin and—from what Matthew could see—continued down his torso. What little could be seen of his forearm was lined with tendrils of red. Matthew put a palm on the door and attempted to push it, stopped only by Aften's objection: "No, what the f—" Aften coughed. "— Matt, I'm not wearing anything."

"Dude, you look like you're dying, let me—"

"It's a nosebleed," Aften very obviously lied, "don't worry. It's a really bad one but I'm just trying to clean up and," Aften sounded exasperated, "and now there's blood all over the floor that I've gotta clean, and—"

"I...are you *sure*, Aften?" Matthew knew he wasn't sure; no nosebleed of his or anyone else's ever produced a smell so pungent. "Because I ca—"

"Oh my God, Matt, I'm okay; can I please—" he coughed; he coughed again. "—please just clean up? You're literally only giving me more work to do right now." Without waiting for a response, Aften abruptly shut the door.

His roommate paused, then knocked again, noticeably more force behind his fist. "Aften!"

"I promise Matt, I'm fine."

Matthew's concern was replaced with anger and again he knocked—though this time "hammered" would be more appropriate and attempted to force the locked doorknob. "Open the goddamn door."

There was no response.

"I said open the door!"

Again, Aften remained silent.

"It's a nosebleed." Matthew replayed the flagrant lie in his mind. *Does Aften think I'm fucking stupid?* However, while not necessarily stupid, he was completely unprepared for a situation such as this. Matthew paced the length of the hallway once, twice, before pausing again at the door, opening his mouth, and then expelled a heavy and solitary breath before returning to Heather. "I don't know what to do."

Jessíka threw on Ethan's sweatshirt and Sara's ballcap (on which was emblazoned some sports logo she didn't care about) and stretched in the seafoam light. Mercer was seated at Sara's vanity, borrowing ("borrowing") her nail polish to shade his fingertips a soft mauve tint. "So. How was Ethan? He learn anything new?"

"Nah." She stood and stepped into a pair of leggings. She accidentally ripped the knee of one—"God*dammit*." —but that didn't necessarily pose an issue. She shrugged, and Mercer nodded in affirmation, "I think it looks good. You're truly a punk now."

"Damn right."

"Ethan sure seemed pissed earlier."

"Yeah." She did not offer anything more.

Mercer finished his nails, gingerly blew on them before shaking them and swiveled around in the chair.

Jessíka huffed. "Why are you doing your nails in here?"

"My light is busted."

"Change the bulb."

Mercer shrugged. He didn't seem keen on acknowledging anything that required effort. "Ethan is not happy Aften's coming."

She was lacing her Converse. "He's my friend regardless."

Unsure of which *he* to whom she referred, Mercer simply nodded. "Yeah. Well, it really messed Aften up for a while; if anyone has the right to be mad, it isn't Ethan."

The room smelled like eucalyptus and semen. This led to Jessíka rifling through the nightstand, from which she grabbed a small cone of incense. She lit it and set it on a magazine as Mercer continued to complain about their housemate: "He can't be a little bitch about the problems he creates for himself. If he isn't happy Aften is here then *he* can leave."

"As long as they don't fight I really don't care," she reiterated. "You coming downstairs?"

Mercer groaned, leaning back. He played with the neckline of his shirt, fanning his chin—the room was still humid with sex, and he personally did not like Jessíka's choice in incense: she'd chosen a soft *forest-y*, rain-scented combination. He'd have preferred something more sweet—

vanilla, or maybe lavender. He shrugged internally; it wasn't his room so he didn't argue it.

Jessíka grabbed an orange bottle and rolled it between her fingers. Mercer watched as she reached towards its cap, paused, and instead set it back down. He stayed quiet. Her medicinal choices were not his business.

Both descended the too-narrow steps in single-file (it was an old house) and joined their housemates: Jessíka fell into the couch next to Sara, who promptly threw her arm across her girlfriend's shoulder. Mercer grabbed the remote and began flicking through channels until whatever half-second he saw caught his attention.

"Wait, wait," Jessíka tapped Mercer's hip. "Go back."

He flicked back—it was a show about cats. Nothing particularly special, though mindless and cute. Mercer looked at her with a disappointed tilt in his eyelids.

"What, they're precious."

He sat the remote down wordlessly and took residence next to her, laying his legs across both her and Sara's laps. Ethan continued cleaning.

The *meowww*s sounding attracted Sara's (rather territorial) cat to the room with a bristled tail, which Jessíka gently prodded with her foot. "Bad Saphi, bad."

Sara laughed and looked behind Jessíka's shoulders to see Mercer. "Dude, you know my mom still to this day thinks her name is short for Sapphire?"

"She's in denial." Jessíka contributed. "She sure does love your 'roommate' though."

"Can't understand why." Mercer chimed in.

Jessíka softly punched Mercer in the shoulder.

Sara clicked her tongue at Saphi. "My little 'weaver of wiles.'"

"That was Aphrodite," Jessíka interjected. Sara waved her hand dismissively.

Ethan relaxed his shoulders in what could only be described as "forcefully" before turning to the couch. "This is your house too, you guys."

Tension.

Mercer picked up a book and pretended to read it.

The remaining two stared at Ethan, but per usual, Sara was the only one to retaliate: "It is literally only my house."

The two locked eyes longer, Sara's deadpan expression, Ethan's reddening one. He licked his teeth—mouth closed, tongue rolling beneath his upper lip—before he lowered, shook his head, and walked into the kitchen.

Aften slammed the door and stumbled back to the bathroom counter. There were splotches of blood everywhere but he paid them little notice now. His initial desire to keep the bleeding contained had since been discarded, thanks to Matthew's interruption. He was unsure of exactly how much he'd lost, but between stubbed toes and a both euphoric and disorienting dizziness, his concern now was instead not to lose any more. Clenching the bronzed washcloth in his fist, he dragged it across his face, smearing pink lines into his cheeks, down his neck—"dammit" —it wasn't cleaning anything.

His arm pulsed in agony, though the bleeding itself had begun to slow. He dabbed the wound, wincing at the touch, and slowly sopped the thickened coagulate. There was an emptiness brewing inside him: a hollowness echoed in his torso and he could only bring himself to sigh as he realized that not *only* had he failed to kill himself, he made a fucking mess of it. His eyes were glossy in the mirror and—something twitched; something small, furred—he threw his head around.

There was nothing in the corner.

...shaking his head, Aften returned his attention to the injury. Thankfully, there was gauze beneath the sink, in a first-aid kit they had until-then used exclusively for bandages—he layered the entirety of his forearm in the tan fabric, breathing between his teeth as he leaked through the first layer, then some through the third, but at the fifth encircling he could no longer see any mark of the soft brown wellspring.

There was rust staining in his messy hairline. Aften ran his fingers through and shook his head; it remained messy, though less incriminating, only slightly more unkempt than usual. *Whatever.* There was a ringing in his ears, and in the distance he could hear the muffled worry of Heather and Matthew trying (and failing) to argue quietly.

He reached for his underwear from the floor, one leg now soaked, though as he pulled them on he paused: *am I okay?*

He wasn't entirely sure what he was supposed to be feeling, but surely...something? He stared at the smears along his unbandaged arm, then to the encased one, to his feet, wet still in the floormat—the knife was still laying in the shag. It had no apologies to offer.

Soon, Aften was beating his temples with his palms. *What is wrong with me, what is wrong with me?* Why was everything normal? Why was he *acting* like everything is normal? Cleaning his face, drying his hair; *why don't I feel anything?* It was a bizarre awareness. Earlier, on the couch, he knew how he felt—or didn't feel—and he was resolved in it, in *knowing* that he felt empty without plausible explanation, but now—now—he knew not only that he felt nothing but that he *should* feel something—or at least he thought he did?—*what was that?*—and that where before there was an emptiness that could kill him there was now an emptiness after trying that could not and he knew no way to absolve himself of this pain without risk yet again of failure, of bloody failure.

The sink was a porcelain pool of hair and pink, grumbling as Aften wrung a washcloth tight above it.

"What?" he looked at himself. His reflection did not reply. "What, am I supposed to act like this never happened?"

There was a knock, to which Aften turned, but did not reply.

"Hey, Aft?" it was Heather; there was a quiver in her voice. "We're going to a party later. Did you want to come?"

Matt had to have told her, he thought. Her response confused him—he expected...well, anything else really. The same frustrations Matthew had earlier? Her tone was that of concern, of confusion, but her question felt empty, almost obligatory. Aften couldn't fault her for that—he was equally confused. Aften honestly could not tell whether or not he should feel insulted.

One of Ethan's hoodies was crumpled in the corner, left at Aften's apartment maybe seven or eight months prior. It was about two sizes too big, but he couldn't let Heather see his arm. It wasn't hard to know that the invitation was nothing more than a refusal to leave him alone. He sighed. There was an implicit prioritization of the party that Aften could not shake, but seeing people would probably be good for him, he lied to himself. "Yeah...yeah, I'll go. Let me grab some pants and I'll be ready."

Heather sighed in relief. At the very least, they could keep a closer eye on him now that he was attending.

Belfry worked at the local liquor store, right on the corner of Hargrove and Fourth: McGallough's Liquor—lovingly dubbed Gallow's by the locals. It wasn't an ideal job, but it helped pay the bills (barely). She was leaning one-elbow on the counter, playing with her nails, staring into nothing as the sound of the air-conditioning hummed through the empty aisles. Her hair was a reddish brown wave tumbling over her shoulders, across her face and against her cheeks. She preferred it that way.

It was about six-thirty, another hour and a half to her shift, and she could not have been more bored. Restocking had been finished hours ago, the countertops couldn't be more clean, and there was nothing to sweep since no one had come in. She'd gone ahead and sent her coworker home early. No point keeping them around if one person could handle everything: that's what she'd say when her boss inevitably asked why only she had been servicing the store. She shrugged.

In her head, she back-and-forthed dialogues for a screenplay, one she'd been working on for a long time, but never found time to finish. The only thing keeping her at all tuned in was her desire for Ethan's party after—well, Sara's party, but Ethan had invited her. As with any party, she needed to secure alcohol for it.

She pulled out her phone and texted her brother:

Hey August, you coming to Sara's tonight?

Ye

She sighed. Her brother sucked at texting. **Cool, we need to bring booze. Should I grab some before I get off?**

Nah. I'll get it. Stay put

She smirked. **Thanks dude.**

Belfry slipped her phone back into her pocket and stretched. Another twenty minutes passed, no customers— a waste of time and payroll. Perfect. She shook her palms and breathed heavy, cracking her neck alongside a swaying bounce.

Behind the counter was a panic button, comfortably beneath the second register. Should anything happen, this was the ideal place to be, so Belfry grabbed the broom and made her way to the store's rear coolers, purposely further from said safety. Not long after, there was a *ding! ding!* as the double-doors swung open. "Welcome to McGallough's!"

She turned the corner just in time to see a masked face and a handgun, both facing her. She immediately let the broom fall to the floor, her eyes locked on the shrouded intruder. "Look, just—" she stammered, "Just take whatever it is you want and go, I won't stop you just—just don't shoot me."

He rushed forward, head low, gun pointed straight toward Belfry, his free hand grabbing bottle after bottle from the shelf and shoving it into a satchel at his waist. Beneath his mask, auburn scruff marked his chin. Belfry's knees buckled inward, and she held her head low, dry sobs heaving between rugged breaths.

August whispered: "God you're dramatic."

"Hurry the fuck up." Belfry scolded her brother. "Your robbery has to look convincing, doesn't it?"

"Theatre majors," he scoffed.

She crumpled further. He scooped more vodka into his bag before dashing for the door again, holding his head low, and disappearing into the afternoon.

Belfry curled into a ball on the linoleum, clenching her fist in her hair, body trembling every now and then. This was arguably her least favorite part, just lying on the floor. Feigning shock was the most boring part of any scheme. After about five minutes of suitable panic, she sat back up and straightened her hair, smeared her eyeliner, and shook her head. She was frustrated he didn't diversify his choices in theft.

Ethan stepped outside and let the screen door fall behind him. It creaked and (*THUMP, thump...thump*) slammed into itself just as his own hand slammed against the back porch guardrailing. He picked at the wet, knotted wood, and watched his breath flush white before him in the cold winter air.

He hated fucking Sara.

He hated listening to her, he hated her being right—he appreciated her housing, even appreciated her by proxy, but appreciation did not null the irritation that burned behind his forehead every time he had to listen to her grating condescension. He pulled out his phone, mindlessly flicking his way between two of the many miscellaneous hookup apps that inhabited it.

"Aften?"

"It'll stay green."

Aften, Heather, and Matthew had collected themselves and began their way to Sara's. The three were pooled together in Heather's van—a grotesque 1996 Nissan, but it worked as a car is expected. The back was piled with clothing and picture frames; Aften in the back-passenger, knees pulled to his chest, feet atop the remnants of a disassembled bicycle. His window was pushed open, and the cold air caught the back of his still-wet hair.

Heather felt both guilt and relief that Aften had joined them. *Surely it was better that he not stay home alone, right?* Certainly, the smarter decision would be that none of them go, but Matthew and Heather were ill-equipped to broach the topic with Aften. *What would we even say?* she continued to muse. *If we can't help and he won't talk about it—Matt tried, after all—he should have a distraction for the night. Whatever reason he were bleeding it couldn't be good if he were lying about it, and if he were lying he clearly wasn't comfortable, and if he were comfortable, we as friends—right? —clearly shouldn't push him and—*

She pushed those thoughts aside. "Next light?"

"Uh, gun it; it's about to turn."

While it was Heather's vehicle, Matthew was driving. Aften was quick to notice the pattern of traffic lights: whether they'd stay red, or if oncoming had a turn light. He had always been good at noticing patterns, the math and predictions alongside it, so—naturally—he decided to major in psychology. Two years in and the most emotion he could express was simply that he "sure was doing it."

"Yellow, your call."

Lights didn't mean much here. The roads were narrow and lonesome, the trees the usual company. Occasionally an equally-old car would pass their van, on its way no doubt to an equally-old house. Birds and stars were all the majesty these roads offered. Matthew stopped, and his headlights teased the constant fog of December.

"Whose party is it?"

Heather and Matthew both glanced at each other, neither wanting to be the one to share the answer.

"Fuck, Sara's house?" Aften rasped, "Guys—"

Heather interjected. "You'll be fine, Ethan probably won't be around anyway. He hates parties."

"Yeah but—green, by the way—but that doesn't change that he's—"

Now it was Matthew that interjected. "Shit, we were supposed to bring drinks." This time, Aften remained quiet. They weren't listening.

Heather seemed unphased and stretched forward before turning to face Aften. "No worries Matt." Matthew glanced from road to over-shoulder as he half-watched Heather. She began fumbling below Matthew's seat, shoving aside shoes and garbage until she pulled forth a bottle of Smirnoff.

"Heather what the f—that's half empty."

Matthew rounded a tight, thickly-foliaged corner, and Aften's eyes widened as a car quickly grew nearer to them. Despite his shock, he didn't say anything.

Thankfully, Heather did. "Matt, watch out!"

Matthew slammed on the brakes, but not soon enough.

Sara retreated to the kitchen to finish cleaning where Ethan had abandoned the dishware. Mercer, now, found he was actually engaged in the book he'd picked up (*Vile Bodies*, by Evelyn Waugh—he'd never read it (as it was Jessíka's)), thoroughly enjoying the two and a half pages he read before setting it down and standing. Jessíka had since slithered to the floor to play with Saphi, who responded with a mix of purrs and playful bites. Occasionally, her handler would wince, but the finger remained locked between tiny teeth. Her hair was a pool of deep brown that lazily curtained her features.

"You okay?"

A shrug replied.

"I'm gonna help out Sara."

A second time, a shrug.

Mercer stepped from brown carpet to beige tile to find Sara scrubbing utensils with a much-too-worn sponge. He leaned against the mock-granite countertop, throwing his head back and staring into a dim luminescence. "What's up?"

Sara slammed a spoon against the sink edge; Mercer jumped; the spoon clattered into the basin. "What is *up* is that Ethan literally will argue about the simplest, most *minute*—" she pinched her fingers together and shook them at Mercer. "—most *minute* of requests, I swear to G—" she stepped back from the sink and breathed. "And literally where are you during any of this? Why is it me that regularly has to cradle him?"

"Hey," he held his hands up and stepped forward, calmer than he needed to be, more dramatic than necessary, "It's your house. I've told you to kick him out."

She lowered her voice. "You *know* I can't do that." She looked towards the living room archway.

Mercer followed her gaze, swatted at a gnat, and looked back. "Yes, I know, I know, he and Jessíka are friends, but—"

"—but *nothing*," she breathed through her teeth. "If having Ethan around offers her anything at all in the realms of comfort, he's fucking staying." She stepped forward. He stepped back. His jeans caught a towel which pulled the silverware tray to the floor. Metal clattered against tile in a rhythmless, dissonant thunder, and such a storm caught Jessíka's attention. With low effort she asked from the other room, "You guys okay?"

No. "Yes," they both answered in rare harmony.

There was a pause as Jessíka asked no other questions, after which Sara sighed, kneeled, and began sorting the mess. Mercer entertained the idea of disclosing Jessíka's inconsistency with her medicine. It was clear having Ethan around strained Sara, and he couldn't be Jessíka's crutch at the expense of, well, everyone else, but ultimately he didn't know what good it would do. Make them mad at each other? Strain the tensions of the house further? It hurt not knowing how to help his friends.

Mercer sighed then leaned down to help, and the two soon after began preparing whatever miscellaneous snacks they had.

Thankfully, the impact was minor. While a very evident impact was made, there was enough time between awareness and braking that, as the car ahead inched forward, the white-blue smudge left by Heather's van certainly proof of their folly, clearly no functional damage had been done.

Matthew held the wheel with both hands as wide-eyed and heavy-breathed he half-heard Heather practicing caution. "...alright...are you?...car...", et cetera. Aften sat quiet in the back seat, staring forward with glazed eyes and grit teeth. He'd braced himself with both arms, his left now moaning below the flesh, nerves daggering atop bone and prodding tendons—he rested his head atop his knees and let out an exasperated lie: "I think I'm alright."

Heather turned back to Matthew. "I don't have insurance."

"Are you kidding me?"

"It's a piece of shit car."

"Their car isn't!"

"Guys—"

"You have open vodka in here."

"Quick, Aften, hide this."

"What—I mean, but—" She shoved the bottle into his hands.

"Matt," Heather strained. "Figure this out."

Matthew nodded, took a deep breath, and Aften watched as his initial look of tensed worry gave way to a much calmer expression. As he exhaled, it seemed his anxieties followed the air from his body and he was replaced with a man made of nothing but composure. He stepped from the van and hurried to the driver side window, theatrical concern clear on his face. Heather and Aften hurriedly rolled their windows down—while the anonymous driver was speaking too quietly to hear from their distance, Matthew's voice carried well.

"Oh my god, are you alright?"

The other driver's answer could not be heard. Aften watched the trees sway around them, a crowd of deep greenery.

"No, no, you're absolutely right—this was *completely* my fault."

"What the fuck is he doing?" Heather gasped.

Aften did not reply. He knew Heather didn't want to hear it. A squirrel stared at him from the trees.

"Of course, I understand, I can grab my license."

Wait...is that a squirrel? Aften blinked. Heather clicked her tongue in audible frustration. Aften squinted. He shivered and his arm burned.

Matthew made it halfway back before locking eyes with Heather, winked, and turned back around. "Actually," he pointed behind Heather's van, "I'm really worried about that blind curve we caught you on." A few meters ahead there stood a church— "would you be okay if we handled this there? I really don't want either of us to get hit, same as this."

Heather watched a few nods. Aften watched a few branches; they intertwined with one another in a brushing, hushed symphony of wind. Curious eyes followed the leaves and from the shadowed depths stepped forth a gaunt-legged creature. Its eyes—no...its one eye—returned Aften's gaze, raising one appendage—paw? talon? —to its gray chest, much as a cat might lift its paw to groom itself. Aften's heartbeat began to dampen the wind as the stress dampened his forehead—he felt himself sweating beneath the hoodie and fanned its collar, feeling a sweltering heat wash over him despite the piercing cold.

His trance was interrupted by a slamming door; startled, he turned to the driver's seat to see Matthew buckling in. Aften hadn't heard Heather, but he could assume well-enough that she had asked what was happening. Matthew pointed to the church. "We're meeting in the parking lot." There was a lilt in his voice that betrayed any honesty.

Matthew turned the key in the ignition. Aften turned towards the woods. The branch was empty of its resident. He shuddered, and his arm whispered agonies beneath the skin. Trees began retreating as they drove. As the sedan they'd hit drove left into the gravel driveway, Aften caught sight of its driver: an older woman, hands thinning on the wheel, hair waterfalling from white to slate to brown, canthi sagging behind large glasses.

And this was the last sight of her Aften had, for as soon had her rear tires met the gravel, Heather's van roared to life at Matthew's command and from ten miles to thirty to sixty-five had they abandoned the old woman before she could so much as reverse in the dusty driveway.

Aften sat forward. Everyone sat quiet.

Jessíka watched Saphi's ears flick; the cat quickly stood and darted from the room, after some unknown victim, some foreign curiosity. As the cat ran, Jessíka's eyes caught sight of something below the sofa—a pocket knife. Unsure of whose, she shifted lazily until it was in her pocket.

She did not want to be here. Not the party—though that was included—but...*here*. "Here" as all places, "here" as being. Everything felt so heavy, so heavy all the time. Sara was in the kitchen preparing for a party Jessíka did not care for, but she could not fault Sara for that. Sara *had* asked her if it was okay, and Jessíka, wanting her girlfriend to enjoy the night, told her of course a party was fine. *Stupid.*

The worst part was not knowing the reason. Any reason. Any reason she felt the way she did beyond an indiscriminate depression that ravaged her mind. She had a partner that loved her, a social group, a home. Even with these, her brain refused her happiness, and that perpetual guilt only tormented her more. She tried to care in the best ways she could, yet nothing ever felt like enough. Even now, lying on the living room floor, just existing near others felt like work—still, she tried anyway. Truly, the worst part of such a pained mind was the constant battle of people caring for her and her being unable to care about anything at all.

Slight tears began to form, whether of sadness or emotional obligation she could not say. It wasn't fair to say she didn't care about anything. Jessíka cared for Sara, she did—*I do.* —but even that level of care did not feel...right. *How do I achieve a standard I cannot even define? What could I do? What can I do?* Questions without answers beyond deprecation clawed their way to the forefront of her thoughts until, unable to tolerate or answer them anymore, she retreated, and again the world and emotion became empty.

Water was running in the adjacent room; she listened to the inane conversation on the television; she scraped the top of her foot against the couch cushions. She wanted to go to bed, but her thoughts were too heavy to carry upstairs. The carpet was comfortable enough.

Gallow's had closed early for the day after the police came to make their report. They questioned Belfry, who answered in messy-haired hysterics and smeared eyeshadow; she wiped her eyes with her palm while responding with gasps, occasionally with words between them. She was clearly in distress, decided the officers, and after the store owner arrived on the scene, he took over the more procedural concerns regarding the security cameras, store policies, and so on. When he angrily asked Belfry why she was the only one present, she stifled her sniffling and said, "No point keeping them around if one person could handle everything, I thought." Her boss pinched the bridge of his nose. An Officer Lewis collected her contact information and soon dismissed her.

Once in her sedan, Belfry fixed her bra, tousled her hair, and began checking her teeth in the rearview. She didn't want to be late.

The sky was gloomy and her makeup a mess, but she would be among friends, and the smudges would make for a good story, at the very least. Her car struggled to start until she repeated her ceremonial cursing, and with a groan it came to life. She left the lot and preemptively silenced her phone in anticipation of her boss's inevitable phone calls. She shrugged—he could threaten to fire her Monday.

The ride was simple enough; Belfry patted the dashboard after every successful acceleration. She wished Aften were with her so she could know when she actually needed to brake. At first it worried her (and the rest of their friends), and they remained apprehensive to trust how he supposedly knew the patterns of traffic lights, but after weeks of accuracy and later months they learned that even without explanation, he never faltered. Curiously, she wondered if August would beat her to Sara's, and whether or not she should stop for mixers, considering her brother had only grabbed vodka. Part of her simply hoped Sara would have some (especially since her paycheck would be cut short this week, considering her shortened hours post-burglary and all), but the other part of her knew Sara better than to expect that.

She sighed. Shots would suffice.

Before her, she slowed to a yellow light, and no sooner had it switched to red did a dark-blue van speed through the intersection. Belfry recognized both the car (as Heather's) and the familiar haphazard driving (as Aften's direction). *I didn't know Aften was coming.* To...Ethan's place. *This may not be as fun as I hoped.* Ultimately, she pushed any concern to the back of her mind—Sara wouldn't stand for any issues, Belfry assured herself.

Ethan scratched his hip and finished his whiskey. A pair of headlights crept into the part-gravel driveway, inching below a carport and resting next to a dilapidated Jeep. The jeep hadn't been driven in weeks, and either apathy or negligence left it parked in such a state with open windows. The seats were drenched in leaves that more closely resembled mulch, the floor mats were irreparably soaked. Sara consistently implored Jessíka to find the keys and seal the vehicle, which would always be declared as "to be done later."

August stepped from his car (arguably the nicest among their friend group: a 2014 Mustang) and saw Ethan approaching him. August had nothing to say—he was thankful for the help though annoyed that of all possible help it had to be him. August motioned towards Ethan, who stepped over equally wordlessly. While August was not close to Aften, Belfry was; so Ethan injuring Aften made her upset, and by extension infuriated her brother. Ethan had no gripe with August, and the awkward transport of booze seemed the only chance to be even in proximity of August. The two began unloading bottles and bottles and more bottles until Ethan pushed his masculinity aside and resolved, "We'll have to make more than one trip."

August grunted.

Ethan pressed more with maladroit conversation. "How's Belfry?"

August knew that Ethan wasn't genuinely interested in his sister. "Alright. Why do you ask?"

"Haven't talked to either of you in a while," Ethan sighed. "Thought I should ask."

"You could always message." August responded, aware that Ethan would not do so.

"Two-way street, pal."

Enough with the kindnesses, August thought. "Get a job yet?"

Ethan grit his teeth.

"Ah."

Without further response, Ethan picked up what alcohol he could carry and moved to bring it inside. Ethan was however halted by August who unexpectedly put a hand on Ethan's shoulder, leading him to jump.

"Listen Ethan," August began. Ethan looked up at the hulking man, easily five inches taller than Ethan who stood at five-foot-eleven. "I see what you're trying to do. It's okay, really—"

Ethan found that mildly reassuring.

"—it's alright, we don't have to like each other. But thanks for helping." With that, August released Ethan's shoulder alongside a push forward that wasn't forceful enough to be angry, but more forceful than was needed. Ethan took the hint: the conversation was over.

The reassurance faded. Ethan, with more speed, continued toward, then into, Sara's house. He set the bottles on the counter in no particular order. Sara and Mercer had recently finished cleaning, and a fleeting moment of guilt brushed past Ethan, as they were doing the only work that had been asked of him.

"August must be here," Sara said, commenting despite having clearly seen August's car pull onto the property.

"What makes you say that?" Ethan asked with biting sarcasm.

It was Mercer who interrupted with a laugh. "No one else ever comes this prepared to drink." Sure enough, not long after he'd said that, August stepped through the screen door, the familiar *thump!* sounding behind him, at which point Ethan excused himself the living room to avoid any more obligatory sociability, stepping over Jessíka who was still prone on the carpet.

More tires sounded against gravel, this time followed by a knock on the front door. Mercer excused himself to answer it, passing Ethan who was situated on the couch, with evidently no intention to welcome the guests himself. "Jessíka," Mercer said, "Get off the floor."

At this point, the party had officially begun. Nameless faces walked in intermittently—some brought cups, some brought food, the particularly enthused brought home-baked dishes. Others brought their presence and energy along, to whom Sara made clear they better limit what they eat.

Not long after, a blue van with a newly-scuffed front bumper arrived.

| Aften wished he hadn't come. | Ethan wished Aften hadn't come. | Sara wished Ethan hadn't stayed. | Matthew wished Aften were alright. |

| Belfry wished Mercer played better music. | August wished to drink. | Heather wished Sara would handle things. | Jessíka wished everyone would leave. |

Mercer left them to their musings, and the music continued.

August and Belfry were as expected of fraternal twins. While both shared the same Scottish heritage that granted them red hair and pale complexions, the similarities roughly stopped there. August was brash where Belfry was soft-spoken; August was direct where Belfry would skirt topics; August preferred sweat of physical work done well where Belfry preferred the art and elation of convincing theatre. Admittedly, those differences came in handy for getting new perspectives on things, or meeting a new crowd, or robbing liquor stores.

Belfry envied August's name. Not because it was particularly good or meaningful, but because his name was intentional. Their mother, insistent her child have a religious name, gave to her son the name August, shorthand for the saint. To Belfry, however, as her mother began to die under the strain of childbirth, sweating, the doctors recounted to their father how she had blurted "Belfry" before breathing her last breath. This was likely the first religious association she could think of beginning with B before she passed.

Belfry envied August's name.

Where August drank, Belfry opted not to. While she assisted in the robbery of McGallough's, it was for the sake of the party's potluck structure. That, and getting relieved from work early—that was a welcome bonus.

"How're you holding up?" She asked her brother. Both were standing relatively centered in the room, poor dancing present on all sides of them.

"Honestly, pretty alright," he hiccupped. While not dancing, there was an evident nod in his stance. She grabbed his wrist and mock-waltzed with him before he eventually shook her free. She grinned, then saw behind him the kitchen archway, through which a nervous cat leapt off the kitchen counter, sending a mug careening to the side which (thankfully) was stopped from falling to the floor by a pan of *something* that had been brought.

Belfry promptly used this as a means to excuse herself and proceeded to collect the skittish creature. Not without some thrashing, she eventually *shhh'ed* Saphi enough to begin toward the stairs opposite the living room. Ethan and Mercer had earlier pushed the couch out of the way, so it was an easy path through. At such path's end, Belfry saw Aften, reclusive and quiet, though still she was excited that he had made it.

Ethan was having a grand time.

For all his frustrations in preparation, he was quick to find relief in the environment of a party, particularly relief in others. He had recently—read: moments ago—become acquainted with a boy, Ryan. After short pleasantries, as one does after meeting a stranger at a party, the two began kissing passionlessly. It was a welcome sensation—warm, playful, but with the added comfort of being meaningless. Tomorrow morning, Ryan would be an irrelevant memory, but Ethan will have enjoyed the evening.

He knew Aften was present but had not seen him. Considering how modest Sara's house was, this was a legitimate surprise, but one Ethan did not criticize. He had not yet forgiven Aften after breaking his wrist. *He asked for it, he asked for it and let everyone hate me for it, he—*

Enough.

Ethan was going to enjoy the night if it killed him. His history with Aften didn't detract from the fact that he was here. *I'm still here!* And whether that presence was a shallow hope of past friendship rekindling, still he remained. The two had not formally "broken up" —it was more that both mutually understood the relationship had ended after Mercer heard Aften scream and burst into Ethan's bedroom. The two were naked, sweating, nothing unusual aside from Aften's hand being bent completely flat backwards.

That was months ago, and while no one spoke to Ethan of the matter, it was without a doubt spoken among the others. He did not need to hear the conversation to know.

Ethan freed himself of the memory and invited the woman seated beside him to join him and Ryan. She shared her name, which he forgot immediately, and as Ryan kissed his lips so too did she kiss Ethan's neck. A shiver ran through his hair and his thoughts ran from his mind.

The air was stale and smelled like smoke, sweat, and casserole. All around Mercer, bodies awkwardly shuffled with red cups in their hands and little enthusiasm in their voices. August was already pouring whiskey and cola into novelty shot glasses of Sara's—some covered in palm trees, others with gas station logos; one had a unicorn on it (Jessíka's), another shaped like a penis (Mercer's). Sara found fun in sharing stories of her travels as people noticed the different glasses—

"What'd you do in Florida?"

"Just visiting friends, enjoying the beach."

"How was Reno?"

"We won three hundred bucks, which bought us the plane tickets home."

"Wow, when did you guys go to Venezuela?"

"Oh, my girlfriend's got family over there."

—despite all of her shot glasses having been collected from local thrift stores. Jessíka of course knew these tales to be false, but she never called the stories into question. Sara liked to create a good time, thrived on it, liked to be interesting—she just wasn't. She was kind though stern, she strived to keep peace, she had a knack for becoming friendly with nearly any soul she encountered. Among all her qualities, however, worldly was not one of them. Her recounted stories were fun, but ultimately untrue. What better way to captivate people than throw parties? To be engaging via proximity to others. Such was Sara.

Jessíka could not help but feel that it was her fault. *Sara works...so much. Once the Jeep is drivable, I can find work, then Sara can take time off, then she can do what she wants to instead of taking care of me... then...*

Jessíka cut herself off: *not again, not now*, she thought to herself. *I'm here to have fun. At least I should be.*

August handed Sara a cup, from which she swallowed without question. Sara promptly gagged, recalling now that August had a vastly different standard of how much whiskey belonged in a mixed drink. While Sara cleared her throat, August had a new, whimsical sway to his dancing.

Jessíka redirected her attention to the music and let Mercer's poorly organized playlist distract her. He had prepared his stereo system earlier in the evening (in which "prepared" means to have lazily hooked up a laptop), from which was now blaring song after song, running from classic hip-hop to hardcore trance just to cycle back into some comfortably familiar Tame Impala.

Aften shuffled in the corner and saw up the stairs, smiling at Saphi who half-peered past the wall, eye reflecting metallic green in the dim hallway light. Aften *tsk tsk tsked* his tongue, but received no response beyond a persistent and unmoving stare. He took a deep drink of whatever concoction August had made him.

Ethan was seated on the couch in the far end of the room; perched atop him, a boy shaking a small bag. Ethan quickly pushed his hand down and glanced at Sara, who hadn't seemed to notice, too engrossed in her fables. Aften assumed him to be Ethan's new infatuate and furrowed his brow, stepped forward to confront Sara, then stepped back into place. He didn't want to cause trouble—Matthew and Heather would have to leave too and that wouldn't be fair to them.

Belfry walked up and stood beside Aften, who rather than look to her remained fixated on the happenings of the living room. "How are you doing, man?"

It would be fine. It would be fine. In forty-five minutes, after enough drinks and with a hard dick, Ethan would steal away with this nameless, one-sixty-pound boy to the bathroom where they'd powder their noses on filthy enamel before returning to the group and being incapable of masking their deviancy. At which point, Aften reasoned, he wouldn't have to be the one to ruin anything. Ethan could do it himself.

"It's been a while since I last saw ya," Belfry continued.

His eyes wandered and he saw Heather and Matthew dancing (poorly) below flashing red lights. Aften liked Heather—she kept Matthew grounded. And when Matthew was grounded, so too did he keep Aften. Heather and Matthew were set to get married in about six months and Aften was excited to be the best man.

An awkward silence lingered before Belfry tilted lightly on her heels and pressed further. "Things have been going well. Still work at the same place, yeah. Thinkin' about going back to school, even if my scholarships are gone."

Or...was he? Sound began to fade—just earlier he had flirted with dying. *How excited could I truly be?* he wondered—*I hadn't even considered the wedding.* Such thoughts led further to doubt: was he selfish? Surely he couldn't be, he told himself—not in regard to his own body, his own life, his choices and life (and death) and autonomy and right as a being to be or not be as he so saw fit. Was he less of Matthew's friend for wanting to die?

Aften allowed his thoughts to deviate from suicide. He turned to Belfry, in whose arms was a very unhappy cat—a cat he was almost certain he had just seen atop the stairs. Saphi rumbled a low growl behind an unmoving mouth, framed by folded ears. Aften rationalized that, being a cat, she had to have just snuck by without him noticing. Her tail flicked, but she seemed accepting (though angrily) of her position in Belfry's hold. Aften blinked, staring at the cat, back to the second-floor hallway—now empty of the Saphi Aften saw (thought he saw?) —then back to Belfry and her hostage. Aften shook his head, startling the cat, who thrashed and writhed until release and ran from the two to disappear up the penumbral staircase. Belfry spoke up, checking her forearms for collateral scrapes. "I'm surprised she let me hold her that long. She almost knocked some stuff over in the kitchen so I had to get her out of there." She followed through with an insincere laugh.

No...that couldn't have been right. Saphi had just been looking down at him...right? Had she been holding him the whole time?

"Yeah," Belfry further responded to nothing, "I don't think anyone actually knew if you were going to be here or not. You alright, Aft?"

Aften ignored the question. He instead finished the rest of his drink. "I didn't know if I was going to be here either."

Jessíka, having moved from the carpet to a plush armchair, watched the party from the room's corner. Her fingers dangled over the sides, playing with the scratches Sara's cat had etched into the upholstery. Bodies shuffled to and from the kitchen, and by the stairs she saw Aften and Belfry talking. She was both envious of the conversation and relieved to be no part of it. Her desire to talk to people was overwhelmed by the obligation to continue doing so once she began. Instead, she resigned herself to a position as a wallflower. Chairflower. She snickered at her own, stupid joke. The room was easy to decipher.

Mercer constantly fidgeted with his chest, adjusting his shirt when he thought no one was looking—his binder must have been causing him trouble. He'd only recently gotten it, and she was proud of him for having done so.

August was thrashing his head to music harder than usual—he'd clearly already drunk himself dizzy, despite it barely being eight o'clock. Four drinks usually got him to this point, but he would be downing more well before the night was out. At his size, it somehow always caught everyone off-guard just how much August could drink and remain coherent. She liked August and his somewhat brutish nature. He never said anything he didn't mean, and while sometimes that may come off as rough, she considered the honesty respectable.

Sara was being her usual beautiful self, checking her makeup in her phone's camera, then smiling at a picture Jessíka knew to be of the two of them, as it was her phone's background.

Ethan was mouth-deep in some boy she knew only as someone else's passing boyfriend (irrelevant) while some girl (also irrelevant) had her fingers exploring the space between Ethan's thighs. Jessíka laughed. She knew the boy was named Ryan and knew he was uninteresting to detriment, though admittedly attractive. Ryan was certainly aware, for any time she had spoken to him in the past (albeit briefly) he had made no effort to have any sense of personality. Ethan's fondling of him was more to aggravate Aften than anything else, at whom Ethan made the occasional glance that he wrongfully assumed no one had seen. She could tell—he was barely hard. It was not difficult for him to become so; Jessíka knew firsthand. The nameless girl looked frustrated. A friend-of-a-friend, maybe? Jessíka didn't give it much more attention. It didn't matter. She didn't matter.

Heather and Matthew were being cute, talking and laughing while holding hands, all smiles. Such ordinary pleasantries bored Jessíka. She set her judgement aside. At least they found pleasure in something. She instead experienced feeling *less* bad—caught between states of sadness or vacancy. Her pills made her ill.

Jessíka loved her friends in what ways she could, truly—she just had a difficult time with the concept of love as a whole. It was so fleeting and specific. She was aware of love's idea, its shape, often shaped like Sara, yet it remained forgotten, too abstract to recall with any certainty. Jessíka sighed.

Belfry was talking to Aften. Saphi leapt from Belfry's arms and ran up the stairs, where Aften's gaze followed and remained. Belfry was consistently readjusting her hair, brushing it behind an ear, then again, then again; it was a red mess.

Aften seemed not to notice. He instead was fixated on something beyond Jessíka's view. He answered questions without looking at Belfry, Jessíka wasn't sure she'd seen him blink. Aften was often quiet, but never this inattentive. She watched him, watched him move—he twitched, shifted, rubbed his arm far too much and failed to hide a wince at each motion. He was in Ethan's hoodie, she recognized— *he'd not have put that on among other options.* His hair was twisting in any direction one could imagine and—with intent squinting—Jessíka saw the rusty brown crust below each of his fingernails. *Hmm.*

There was a flush of envy.

The room was easy to decipher. She did well with such, reading people; which is how Jessíka could tell he had clearly tried to kill himself earlier that afternoon.

Whatever Belfry was saying, Aften could tolerate none of it. He didn't want to be alone at home, but at the same time felt he shouldn't have come. The music was too loud, the lights were too bright, his arm hurt, his stomach was swimming; everything was overstimulating, and Aften needed an escape. Ethan had since relocated, and while seeing him had been agonizing, being unaware of when he might see Ethan *again* somehow felt worse. Belfry rested her arm on Aften's shoulder, but he swatted her away. He felt himself speak, but did not know what he said, and without another look he made his way up the creaking stairs. The beats and lights grew softer behind him.

The first door to his left—the nearest choice, and therefore the most reasonable one. He knew it to be Mercer's room. He reached for the lightswitch—flick, *flick*; flick, *flick*—but as was traditional Mercer fashion, it did not work.

Aften locked the door behind him and sunk to the floor, head in his hands, nursing a headache with his forefingers. There was a soft chittering noise itching behind the resonant party below. As the pulsing behind his eyes began to fade, however, the chittering did not. He lifted his head, and there, staring directly at him, one appendage pulled to its breast just as before, was a single-eyed gray beast growling in the weak December moonlight.

"Hey, how've you been?"
"I've been."

"Have you heard from Titus recently?"
"No—no one seems to be able to get a hold of him."

[unintelligible]

"Where's Parks?"
"Said his boyfriend is sick
so he's staying home."
"Aww, that's sweet."

"I'm going to punch him in his fucking throat."
"*Shh, shh*—he's right there."
"I don't—!"

"Is Aften okay?"
"Not sure. He's not been
answering my texts."
"Mine either.
"I hope he's alright."
"Yeah."

[unintelligible; angry]

"—so she's seeing a psychiatrist now."
"Good, I'm proud of her."

"I literally don't know their name, they go by
[unintelligible] and—"
"Then that's their name."
"I mean their *real* name."
"That is—"

"I think I'm
seeing things…"

"Having a body
is exhausting."

[unintelligible]

[unintelligible; laughing]

"Did you try the little sandwiches I brought?"
"No, I'm not super hungry."

"I don't know why I'm here."

"I think my nose is bleeding…?"

"My bird died last week."
"Oh no, I'm so sorry."
"Don't be. Thanks, but don't be. Things die."

"Freud doesn't deserve the credit he gets."

[laughter]

"Who invited her?
"Sara obviously. It's her party."

"Do you believe in God?"
"—we'll die regardless."

[unintelligible]

[unintelligible; laughing (fake)]

[unintelligible]

[unintelligible]

[unintelligible]

[unintelligible]

It was rather annoying, Sara thought, how inseparable Heather and Matthew were.

The two were clearly happy, and for that she too was happy, but the inability to interact with one without the other grated her. That wasn't to say she would not want to interact with both, but something about the inability to function except in direct relation to another irritated her greatly.

It seemed she could not place why. She redirected her stare to Jessíka, whose stare seemed pointed nowhere at all.

Matthew and Heather were oblivious to Sara's position, and as such continued to enjoy their night. With each drink Mercer's music seemed to get better, though Heather limited herself. Matthew drove them here, she figured it only fair that she should drive them back home. As she (poorly) danced, she took in the art on the walls, the statuettes people strove to avoid knocking with their elbows, the dust Ethan failed to successfully clean that began to dance with them. A few people coughed. Mercer and Matthew were chatting over the music, but the conversation was broken to Heather. She caught brief mentions of sports (that Mercer quickly derailed) and comments about photography (which Matthew quickly derailed). After so much of this, Heather realized she did not have interest in the conversation. She knew of Mercer, but not so much knew him. It was Matthew that had been invited, after all.

No matter her attempts at distraction, there was a soft guilt pressing inside her. She saw Aften standing in the corner, talking with—or more accurately, listening to—Belfry as his glazed eyes pointed elsewhere. He was fanning the collar of Ethan's hoodie (which Ethan had seemed yet to notice) and while it was starting to get mildly humid, Heather did not think it hot enough to rationalize just how much Aften seemed to be reacting. *Is he okay?*

She knew the answer was no, but internalizing it provided a sense of absolution. She cared, or at least performed care, and that had to be enough.

Unwilling to confront that thought any further, she looked to August, who at this point in the evening was looking much rougher than when she'd seen him upon entering. His previous sways turned into wholly off-beat spasms, and he inconspicuously was clutching his stomach. She tapped Matthew on the shoulder and pointed to August. "Yeah," Matthew began, snickering, "That seems about right."

No longer distracted by Mercer, Matthew now tapped Heather in return, nodding to the couch just as Ethan and a boy Matthew did not recognize escaped through the kitchen archway. "Who was that?" he asked.

Heather was not sure. "So long as he keeps Ethan distracted, I'd consider him a friend."

August clutched his chest and closed his eyes, soon after forcing them back open. Shutting them only thrust the room into black motion, and his stomach could not afford anything but stillness. He made his way to the kitchen. Still loud, but less active; here he could lean against the counter and make the intelligent decision to pacify his churning stomach with tiny dollar-store hors d'oeuvres. They were dry. He washed a choke down with a swig of 80 proof theft.

It had been a few hours since the party began, and among all the conversation August's favorite company had been the alcohol (in particular, his stolen vodka; something about larceny just added to the charm).

There was a glimmer below the kitchen sink. Through squinting eyes, August decided it was a knife. Why it was abandoned there, he was unsure, but even in his stupor he wished for either safety, cleanliness, order, or some combination that inclined him to pick it up. Such was a mistake.

As he leaned down to grab the utensil, all the nausea pooling in his gut tipped forward, as though he were a tilting carafe of acid. August grunted. "....aw hell." Immediately he leaned back up, knife no longer his focus, and turned to rush from kitchen to hallway to bathroom before his body expelled itself. The door was locked, but old—as such, it gave way to August's bullrush with ease, much to the dismay of Ethan, who was pressed against and inside a stranger atop the bathroom countertop. Both paused their thrusting—aghast. "August, what the hell!"

August ignored him, pressing his hand against his back and shoving by to the toilet, which he promptly retched into, porcelain gargling eviscerated echoes into the cramped half-bath. Ethan swiftly reached forward and shut the door again, trapping the vomiting intruder with them.

"Do you mind?" Ethan's nameless fuck asked.

August waved his hand and coughed again. "Don't stop on my behalf."

The two blinked.

"That was rhetorical—"

"I'm vomiting, asshole!"

The shout urged more burning liquid from him. "Go...go to a fucking *bedroom* if you insist on harassing Aften."

"Hey—!"

"Hey *nothing*." August was having none of it. The obligatory kindness from their driveway dialogue had since faded in light of Ethan's infuriating entitlement. "You're not clever. You're not cute. You fucked Aften up and now you can't—" a threatening burp, a pause; August continued, "—and now you won't just admit you were completely in the wrong."

"Hey!" This time, the stranger.

Whether it was the alcohol, unfettered anger, the interruption, or his illness, a sudden and active irritation overtook August, who stood and shoved his hand forward, around the neck of the unfamiliar guest, and pressed his head sharply into the mirror. August felt a heartbeat pulsing through his neck. "You. What's your name?" Ethan was wide-eyed and struck still. He was glad that August had chosen to direct his anger in a direction other than his.

A gulp. "My name is Ryan."

"Well, Ryan," August groaned, clenching his eyelids, "I need you to stop speaking." August was easily twice the size of both of them. It was no secret August was not a fan of Ethan, and by extension not a fan of Ryan. Despite it all, Ryan remained erect. August felt inclined to hold tighter.

August turned to Ethan, who had long-since pulled free from Ryan and was now fastening the drawstring of his pants. He leaned in. "What's your problem?"

"Your breath is vile."

"Your attitude is vile."

Ryan shuffled, to which August tightened his grip. "The only reason you have a place to live is because of Jessíka, you know that? Sara is closer friends with Aften than she'll ever be with you, yet you insist on an... oh, what's the word—*antagonizing!* —antagonizing her friend. Tell me why that is."

Unsurprisingly, Ethan did not tell August why that was.

"So be it." August shrugged. "You'll never be with Jessíka so long as Sara is in the picture, but you need her in the picture to have anywhere to live, you fucking leech." Ryan didn't do anything, but August locked his grasp tighter to prove a point. At this point Ryan did begin to shuffle until August released him, though Ryan remained naked and silent atop the counter. August's voice was deeper, mildly slurring though intimidating all the same beneath its gravelling rage. "But you still do nothing but fuck and aggravate people. Do you even like Jessíka? Or do you just need a home? Which part are you using her for?"

There was a knock on the door, with the recognizable, rattling irritation that was Sara's knuckles. "What's going on in there—open up."

August wasn't in the mood to combat Sara and as such leaned into Ethan's face before he had time to protest.

Sara pushed the door ajar and saw August pull his mouth away from Ethan's, interrupting what had moments before been a kiss. Ethan furrowed his brows but did not argue, for it was better that Sara thought they were mid-coitus than mid-fight. Ethan tasted the aftermath of August's vomit and stifled recoiling at the sensation while August—realizing his discomfort—sneered at the thought.

Sara was ultimately unphased, though unconvinced. She (and everyone else) knew well that August was never inclined to engage with Ethan more than was socially required. Even so, she asked, "Yo, everything alright in here?" With a cursory skim she noted that nothing in the bathroom seemed broken—*thank God*.

August gave Ethan two short pats on his cheek, which Ethan swatted away. "Nah. Ryan here was just leaving. I need air." He squeezed past Sara and merged with the kitchen crowd, plucked a pair of keys from the doorside hooks, and vanished beyond the screen door.

Sara turned to Ethan, then to the nude figure sitting atop the sink. She did not appreciate a stranger fucking in her bathroom. If anyone were going to fuck in her bathrooms, they damn well better live there.

"Nice to meet you Ryan," she lied. "I'm sure Ethan will show you out."

Heather watched Sara trudge off in response to some loud noise, then turned just in time to see Aften hold his hands up to Belfry and stumble, excusing himself up the stairs. Matthew kissed her neck, then stole the bottle from her hand. She laughed and playfully pushed his chest, leading him to slightly spill his drink. Even beneath his complexion, Heather could see drunken reddening and felt herself growing just as warm with him.

The music had shifted genres innumerable times now, but their casual dancing remained consistent. A few friends passed them by, a few unfamiliar faces, most of which stopped to chat. The two had that personality—welcoming without question, for better or worse. They kept themselves distant though. With the exception of their roommate, they stayed out of the inner machinations of relations between everyone. It was no secret Ethan was on everyone's bad side. Everyone appreciated Sara, if in weird ways—she was like the group's mom, always keeping things as in-control as she could. She wasn't the best at it, but she tried; Heather kept it succinct, describing her as "bitter but well-intentioned."

Heather and Matthew enjoyed the parties but were looking forward to moving after their coming marriage. Part of each of them worried about losing their friends, while the other parts were—almost with apprehension—thankful to be away from them. It felt wrong to want to be separate, but too often it felt as though they were in a limbo of *wanting* to be friends without actually passing the threshold.

Jessíka approached them. Before she could say anything, Heather had already embraced her in a hug. "It's so good to see you again! How have you been! How's your writing? How's Saphi?"

Jessíka answered each question in order—mostly lies, hints of sincerity—and smiled. Heather had that effect on people. Matthew was dancing off-beat to the music and pretending he knew the words. His dancing ceased, however, as Jessíka took note of a vehicle driving from the property and prodded Matthew's shoulder, redirecting his attention to the window. Illuminated vaguely by a dim streetlight, a blue van flickered in and faded out of view. "Isn't that your car?"

Aften crawled forward, slowly, intently, eyes locked with eye as...whatever it was pulled its gangly arm back and bared its teeth. Lips folded back, as if peeling away from the bone below it, and needle-point canines glinted yellow in the lowlight. Its skin was scattered with patches of coarse fur as if onset by mange. Aften shivered, to which the creature lunged forward. He stumbled back, and it retreated, having completed its territorial display.

Full of alcohol and curiosity, self-doubt and impulsion, Aften pressed onward, this time leaning on his knee and extending an arm. With each blink, the creature seemed to vanish, returning only when its eye again became visible—a physical avatar of impermanence: a living, aggressive irony. Where a second eye might have once been was just a black, empty void, as though darkness were watching him. It couldn't have been any larger than a small dog, though it seemed to ebb and flow in size as its penumbral outline shifted with each swaying step. It stepped side to side on three spindly legs, a fourth one held to its chest as an injured animal might. Aften's heart throbbed in his neck and his muscles became stiff—his fingers twitched as if calcified by disquiet, though this time when the foreign beast charged towards him he retained composure, surprising even himself. He felt his blood pounding in his ears, the reverberating bass the floor below growing more muffled as thoughts were overcome by an infantile primitivism; idiocy—he had to know what this thing was.

With a third lunge it aggressed, and with uncharacteristic swiftness Aften swung his fist and caught the beast squarely in the jaw, knocking it against the wall as a dispelled *thump!* was absorbed by the drywall. He was upon it—hands still cold, still stiff, though now around the torso of this formless anomaly. Its colorless fur crept between his fingers, and its teeth reared back and disappeared beneath the fabric of Aften's hoodie, pressing deep into his skin and tearing with what might it could. It kicked its back feet up and scratched wherever it could land—Aften groaned between struggling breaths, his left arm shooting pain that resonated through him and collected in pools behind his teeth, air pockets of agony bursting with every kick.

Aften had had enough.

He drew back his injured arm, his right fist gripping *wherever* and, as if the limb of a ghost—unfeeling except for a throbbing declaration that it existed only in reception of its gash—Aften punched down into the darkness, fist meeting flesh, fist grazing teeth, fist acting as its own while his eyes adjusted to darkness, to adrenaline. Shadow gave way to outline, to muted color—red began to well beneath light gray fur, a single eye with a pupil so large there was nearly no iris stared up, glaring at Aften, glaring through him, nestling itself deep into him. Aften's teeth were mirrored in the reflection of its glazed eye—he saw himself smiling, his hand growing warmer and warmer, wetter, softer, until soon all it felt was replaced exclusively with force of impact. Each punch sent lightning coursing through his wound, which wrapped itself around bone, fueled a twisted grin; in the reflection he was watching himself—watching—

—*wait*—he was no longer watching himself, he—*fuck*—Aften was watching himself *watch* himself and the grin he had so admired faded behind a grotesque epiphany. He paused mid-swing, unfeeling shifted to trembling, the subtle caress of crawling liquid collected at the base of his wrist. Shallow breaths rose and fell below him, matted fur exhaling life—the creature was slave to its instincts, baring teeth in defiance where any sane creature would seek escape.

Soon the breathing slowed and ceased. And below Aften was the limp and still husk that once was Saphi.

"What was that?"
"What was what?"
"There was a noise."
"I didn't hear anything."
"Hmm."

"Must've been nothing."

Matthew took a moment to notice, but Heather wasted no time shoving herself through the crowd. She pushed the blinds aside in a dissonant clatter and watched as her vehicle slipped into fog. Pushing her way past Belfry, she flung the front door open and stepped to the cool front patio. Her feet were cold against the stone, even through her socks. "What the hell?" She paced, paced more— "What—who took my car!" Jessíka made no effort to follow.

From the back of the living room: "Who left the front door open!" Sara soon emerged, narrowly avoiding a stumble, full cup in hand. "What are you guys doing, you know Saphi could run out. If you're going to smoke—"

"Someone took Heather's car."

"What?" Sara's demeanor shifted from frustration to shock in an instant.

"Someone took my car."

"Shit."

"What?"

"It was August," Sara stated with a sigh.

Both Belfry and Heather: "What!"

"He last took keys; I'm guessing they were yours. I couldn't tell from the hallway."

Heather pulled her phone out, hand trembling. "This is ridiculous, I'm calling the cops."

Matthew threw his hands over her phone. "No, no no *no*, you can't do that. You *cannot* do that."

Heather stared at him in disbelief, then realization settled over her features and she threw her hands up. "You're right."

Sara breathed a cloud of cold white confusion, which dissipated in the night air. Heather avoided her eyes as she provided her explanation. "We hit an old woman's car earlier."

This time, somehow, Sara's breath seemed angrier.

"What!"

"What do you mean '*what*?'"

This was absurd. Matthew slurred ineffective comforts. "All we can— ... all we can do is wait."

Heather turned. "Belfry, call your br—" but Belfry had since withdrawn from the group, likely becoming one with the excited apathy indoors.

Mercer got frustrated and excused himself from the room, just as it seemed everyone else had. A room full of people he did not know, a house full of music he put together to which no one was paying attention. Which was fine, he told himself. No attention is preferable to bad attention, and everyone was too inebriated for anything to be bad. Except for Mercer.

His skin itched below itself and there was a sudden flush of heat that pushed from his core to his fingers, a molten anxiety that painted his vision with static. Everywhere he looked—his clothes, the guests, the knife on the floor, the hallway panelling—existed in doubles and thirds all at once while he made his way to the back porch. He was dizzy. The air was cold and bit into him just the way he needed—quickly. A shiver coursed along his spine; he desperately craved the chill of the evening air.

Everything sucked. This party, his roommates, his body, the cold night air that calmed him, the burning heat that was him, there was nothing in this moment that did not aggravate Mercer to his very core. He shoved his hands against the railings and winced as a splinter found home, then tightened his grip more, more, harder while loose wood pushed and took root into deepening pockets of flesh. Breathing grew slower and harder as a scratch gnawed beneath collar bones and up, up. Lowering his head, his shoulders buckled and lurched while an undulating spine tore itself up, up, following the curve of a back it was abandoning until Mercer's head was pushed down and pressed hard and rough against the coarse backs of his earthy hands. Blood seethed behind teeth while air pockets detonated themselves and Mercer—in a flush of forbidden elucidation—shifted his jaw as—one, two, four—teeth clattered against teeth against tongue against roof against reason.

Fear.

None of this was real, he knew—dissociation was familiar enough but always equally unwelcome. With suddenness, his body felt not itself, not his own. It was merely a vessel, and the vessel was sinking.

He went to bite at—at anything—at the nothing that was present—at the very knowledge that this couldn't be happening only for his lips to fold into themselves, curl backwards, leaving behind a gaping hole that consumed his mouth in reverse, his eyes in reverse, until the darkness of December was replaced with the darkness that was Mercer. Unblinking—incapable of blinking—incapable of seeing yet still knowing—there within him was this feeling that he was wholly outside his body, a violent dissociation he didn't know how to prevent, a consuming absence.

"...Hey," Jessíka said, patting Mercer on the cheek.

With a sudden snap, it seemed as though Mercer's body had completely undone and redone itself in the span of a millisecond. A grounding. He was on a porch, in the night, at a party. Everything was normal. Everything was normal. *It isn't normal though, not really.* He looked to Jessíka with unfocused eyes and heavy breaths. His body was still his body. Only quiet breath and inconsiderate insects filled the gap between them.

Mercer hadn't seen Jessíka step out with him, and admittedly hadn't noticed much of her presence tonight in general.

"C'mon," she said, "It's getting colder. Let's get you inside."

❖ ❖ ❖

Driving felt good. Driving felt like just what he needed.

August gripped the wheel tightly, a hand at both *ten-and-two*, as one is taught. It was dark out (as expected for being past midnight) so August was comfortable if not *not* sober. *It was only a few,* he reasoned (poorly) while he continued to dance between the subdued white and yellow markers of the road.

Soon, however, the reds and blues of a police siren were dancing behind him and suddenly his slight swerving didn't feel quite so slight after all.

Shit...

❖ ❖ ❖

Ethan stomped up the stairs, frustrated at August, at Sara, at Mercer, at Aften—he needed to be alone.

The stairs were too fucking narrow and the hallway was too fucking dark and as Ethan went to use the hallway restroom just to find it locked—*mother f—* —he was resolved in knowing—with Mercer downstairs—that he could comfortably use his restroom without issue. Which only led to his confusion in finding Mercer's door *also* locked.

Ethan blinked. Unsure of what to do next, Ethan blinked again. He had just passed Mercer on the way upstairs, there was no feasible reason for the door to be locked.

He paused, torn. Going downstairs would mean facing Sara again, versus breaking into his housemate's room. He slammed his weight against the door, the choice obvious. The door creaked like most things in the house, but only marginally budged. Ethan rolled his shoulder before withdrawing a cigarette from his pocket and bringing it to life with a match. He held the trembling flame between his fingers, watching it skitter and jump, envying how much life it had, even if fleeting. Raising a foot, Ethan planted it against the door, carefully close to the doorknob, withdrew it, then waited for a comfortable resounding of bass from below to slam the ball of his foot against the plank, which flung open with a splintering grind.

The room was lit the smallest amount by his match as Ethan stepped in. The lightswitch—flick, *flick*; flick, *flick*—*dammit*—did not work, but this inconvenience was made insignificant by the shuffling Ethan heard from the corner of the room. Flinging the match to the side, just in time to see the figure standing, Ethan saw—

"Aften?"

Aften stood, hands behind his back, feet planted firmly against the ground and each other, covering as much of the maimed cat as he could. Thankfully the room was near impenetrable in its shadows but still Aften stammered. He watched as the flame began to creep closer to Ethan's fingers, his features pulled taut and gaunt in the light. Aften held his hands behind his back, tightening them into fists, feeling the dried sanguine memory crack with motion.

"What are you doing here?"
"I needed time alone."
"In Mercer's room?"
"I could ask you the same."

There was a quiet tension. The match did not care. Aften, however, did, and made the first movement to the bed. Ethan's eyes followed, for which Aften was thankful. Saphi's eyes stared off into nothing, at which Aften jerked his head away.

The door softly swung shut behind them and with uncharacteristic command, Aften said "Sit."

Surprisingly, Ethan did. The match began tickling his fingers, Aften saw, yet Ethan did not seem bothered. Aften had learned not to ask. Ethan took a drag of his cigarette.

"Dating was a mistake."

Aften already knew that, but something about hearing it made it worse.

"I'm not sorry."

Aften had known that for a while.

"But we don't always have to regret mistakes. Just know they weren't the best choice. You were a bad choice."

"You're an asshole."

"You're a coward."

"You're a liar."

"You're a parasite."

"You're hot when you're angry."

"You're still a mistake."

"You're still cute."

"Wait—"

There was no waiting.

Ethan shook his match until it was a white wisp in darkness and pressed his thumbs into the recesses below Aften's jaw. His fingers were hot, his grip tight, his breath fermented and bitter. Ethan was nothing but coruscating teeth and deep brown irises that Aften pleaded remain locked on him, that they drift nowhere—stay anchored on him—in him—deep within him as a bad memory always is—that Saphi (the poor creature) stay bloodied and obscured.

Ethan's ashen finger crept into Aften's mouth and played its leaden game with a drying tongue.

"You beat the shit out of me."

"I'll do it again."

"Do it again."

Aften slammed his mouth shut—a grunt from Ethan—a smirk from Aften, a soft warm taste flickering across his senses, a soft growing anger creeping across Ethan's features.

Both smiled.

Ethan pulled his finger free and cupped Aften's face in his palm. It was hot—with fire, rage, or passion Aften was unsure. The two were shades in a room of regret, wraiths wrapped in memories, and as darkness eloped with early decay, Ethan's hand slipped away, curled into a ball, and relentlessly punched Aften in his dim, grinning face.

"Hey Belfry?"
"Yeah?"
Sara seemed distraught. "Have you seen the cat?"

There was no response.
Again: "C'mon. Let's get you inside."
"No."
Jessíka sighed. "Mercer—"
"I said no." He turned, his face pale, his expression empty. He spoke with a stoic resolve, a living stone, the voice of a body that had exhausted itself in merely being. "No," he said again without prompting.

The two stared at each other. Beneath stars, smoke, and sound battled friendship and obstinacy while Jessíka made her decision. "At least let me get you a coat."

As she turned and reached for the door, Mercer's voice cut the air. "Why do you tolerate Ethan?"

Jessíka could not tell if it were the cold, the anger, the self-detriment, or the alcohol bringing this question forward, but never had Mercer been so blunt about his distaste for Ethan. Mercer similarly wondered. Ethan had not done anything in the immediate moment, but he had done enough and Mercer was in just the wrong enough mood to let himself get mad about it. Jessíka found herself at a loss—and when such loss led to more silence, Mercer repeated himself: "Why do you tolerate Ethan? What does he do for you?"

He's... she thought. *He makes me feel less empty? That's not fair. It's true—but not fair. So do—*

"All he does is take—"

I don't have many friends—

"Sara only puts up with him for you—"

That's obvious—

"He's a drain on me and Sara working—"

I said I'll work...once the Jeep is fixed—

"He broke Aften's wrist!"

I'm scared of losing him.

I'm scared of losing someone.

I'm scared of losing anyone.

"I'm..."

The wind toyed with her neck and her teeth shuddered. The air suddenly felt colder. Even after opening the door, the music felt quieter. The taste of anything and everything dissipated into wet nothing stinging her tongue. She closed her eyes and smothered the burning on their edges, the corrosive and honest welling. Then, with nothing else to defend herself to Mercer said, "At least let me get you a coat."

Aften fell backward, but not before grabbing Ethan's collar and yanking him adjacent. Aften's hands felt raw and his arm burned as he pulled the hoodie from his sweat-soaked body. Ethan's eyes widened at the tear in Aften's arm, yet as he opened his mouth to question it, Aften placed a palm against his lips and pulled him close to the comforter, burying his face into Ethan's neck and latching his teeth harshly around the skin. Aften heard a moan, and reached down to feel Ethan hardening between them.

Ethan shuffled to pull his pants down, pulled his dick free of his boxers, then threw himself atop Aften, shoving his arm aside and planting their lips together while winding his hand tightly around Aften's neck with choking pressure. Aften ground his hips upwards, feeling Ethan's cock beneath tightening pants. Mercer's room was dark—it was nearly impossible to see now that the door had shut, save for the smallest sliver of light creeping in from the bathroom door. Ethan smelled like cheap cologne, and Mercer's bedding smelled like cheap lube, the bottle of which was left next to the pillow above them. Ethan hurriedly reached for it and pumped it into his hand while Aften tugged his own jeans off.

The music from the party below pumped through them alongside adrenaline and testosterone—Ethan shoved the thumb of one hand into Aften's mouth, the thumb of the other—now covered in lube—teased his ass before pressing past resistant muscle and sliding in to a chorus of gasps. Aften reached around and dug nails into Ethan's shoulders.

The darkness spun with ecstasy and alcohol as the two kissed and fondled each part of the other with physical apologies—lies? —lies. His foot quivered, leg itched and twitched while Ethan pulled his finger free and pressed himself throbbing atop, against, then inside Aften. He let out a moan, which Ethan promptly smothered beneath a wet hand before pushing forcefully forward—Aften gasped airless against skin. Ethan's breath was hot and smelled of liquor. Aften rolled his eyes back and rocked against the mattress. He could feel the noise its old frame sang, but such was overshadowed by the congregation bleeding through the floor.

His nails dug deeper, and sound gave way to the pounding impression of sound—noises founded only in the knowledge they should be there. He watched Ethan's mouth move and simply nodded, unsure of what was being said. Aften raised his head and bit into Ethan's neck, feeling the gasp escape him while his tongue danced with raised skin. Tastes of iron and saltwater teased the sense of aged incense wafting through the room—Aften could not tell if it were his head or his prostate pounding harder.

The back of his hands tickled—he waved it aside. They tickled again—he grew agitated; he peered past the blurred and rhythmic figure of a sweating Ethan and saw, sitting there atop Ethan's back, unfazed, unblinking, a single eye shining in what little light was available. Aften paused—Ethan did not. Still gasping, Aften reached up and shakingly prodded the creature, empty fear pulsing through him. It did not move whatsoever—no, instead, it simply curled its lipless teeth to reveal what could only be a smile. Aften smiled back, tightening his legs around the thrusting mate.

He resumed his pace, quickened his pace, deepened his teeth and tightened his claws while Ethan's touch commanded the curves of his back, his hips, his collar, soon pressing heavy fingers against his throat in asphyxial bliss. Aften held him closer, Ethan pushing his head roughly against Aften's chin, growls crawling their way from within him. To his left, another eye, then another, as from the shadows stepped forward two creatures, three, six, until the corners and crevices and nowhere and everywhere were an audience of merged, one-eyed figures staring down upon heated coitus.

The mattress was growing damp—Aften could taste blood—his teeth ached through numbness, mouth watered with skin—he could feel Ethan groaning through his flesh but sound was replaced with scent, with touch, with sensation buried within him pushing outward from a deep cavern of heated nothings—nothing mattered. Nothing mattered! And oh! what a revelation such knowledge was! —he gripped tighter, Ethan did so too, each digging nails into the other, rapturous agony surged through nerves as burns danced from arm to back to bone to the primal, apathetic depths of every creature below the sun, and in the darkness Aften's creatures grew closer, and the collective eyes and the thousand mouths descended upon them in the everwarm, everuncaring blackness.

"License and registration."

Hands safely remained on ten-and-two.

A pause. "I said, license and registration."

August slowly grabbed his wallet. "So...I've got my license, but this isn't my car."

The answer did not seem to stir much. "Proof of insurance?"

"One second." He began rummaging through the glove compartment. Surely Heather was more responsible than he was; he took the car for that very reason. He silently praised himself for this choice, for his handgun remained in his car at Sara's. Driving his car more than needed after his *transaction* with Gallow's earlier would have, simply been foolish. "Uhh…"

"Uh?" The officer mimicked.

"I...don't seem to have any."

A second police vehicle pulled to the scene, and the nameless officer stepped aside, holding up a finger with an obligatory "stay here" before stepping away to speak with the newly-arrived associate.

Now August was alone and could panic. His thoughts raced—*what do I say? this isn't my car; how do I get out?* —as he watched in the rearview the two talk for longer than was comfortable before stepping back to their cars where the blinding lights of two spinning police beacons obscured his sight beyond understanding. He fingered the keys, thinking: *this van probably wouldn't beat them.* He definitely would not beat them. Did he feign ignorance? *I mean,* he thought, *I haven't lied in any way yet.*

The new officer approached, this time, her face much more serious than her associate had been. She had the face of someone who would rather be in bed, and the half-raised eyebrow of someone who already knew the answer to the question she was about to ask: "Whose car is this?"

August raised his eyebrow in return. "A friend of mines."

She stepped back, pulling a flashlight from her belt and stepping to the van's front. A cursory flick of the light from one corner of the bumper to the next was followed by a slow, confident step back to the driver's-side window. It made August's palms sweat.

"We got a report earlier about a van matching this description being involved in a hit-and-run. You know anything about that?"

August remained silent.

"And, shockingly enough, this van has white paint all over its front, much like the color of the sweet old lady's car I spoke to after the incident."

Further silence. Faster heart rate.

"I find it rather convenient that you wouldn't share whose car it is, don't have insurance, and are unaware of the crime it was a part of."

"*May* have been a part of," August blurted defensively, "I don't—"

"Cut the bullshit right now." She straightened her posture and stared down the bridge of her nose. For all of August's stubbornness he still found himself stifling a nervous shiver. "Either you know the person, or you stole the car, and we both know which one of those is worse for you. Now, let's give you the benefit of the doubt: maybe you *don't* have anything to do with the crime, but now you're obstructing a police investigation by not disclosing information—"

August wasn't sure that was true but was far too intimidated to argue in the face of alternatively being arrested.

"—additionally," she pointed back to her associate, "I've been informed this car was swerving heavily. So, your options are as follows: either you lie and tell me you stole this car and I treat it like truth; you refuse to comply and we have you take a breathalyzer we both know you'll fail; or, you make an *anonymous tip* about where we may find the owner of this car, take this car there, and we'll let you go for being compliant."

August looked confused, and the officer was clearly able to see that.

"Oh, I know what you're thinking," the officer continued. "'Why not arrest me now?' Or 'Why a hit-and-run versus a DUI?'"

She was intuitive, August had to admit.

"The answer is simple—you're very, very lucky. I've got a soft spot for sweet old women, particularly when that sweet old woman is my mother. Local woman. Never harmed anyone. Been driving that cute little white Lincoln for going-on eighteen, nineteen years now. And if I am in a situation to choose between some shit-face kid or helping my mom, well, then that shit-face kid just happened to be in the right place at the right time. So tell me, of your three options, which do you find in your best interest?"

The night was quiet beyond the sound of bugs and the very rare passerby car. Clouds obscured the light of the moon and wind rustled what few dead leaves remained on the trees. The crisp scratch of asphalt beneath boots grew softer as the officer stepped away from August, who—with no more words, very little breath, and incredibly wet palms—rolled up his window, shifted the van into drive, and, crestfallen, began his drive back to Sara's.

Sara found herself with unpleasant company as Belfry and Heather argued in the living room corner. Matthew, unsure how to resolve such an issue, stole away to the kitchen to prepare for himself another drink, just in time to watch Mercer step inside from the back porch. He prepared a second drink and raised it towards Mercer, who drank it eagerly, disregarding Matthew's attempt at cheers.

"What were you doing outside?"

"Getting some fresh air."

"Did it help?"

Mercer ignored the question. "Where is everyone?"

Matthew aimlessly waved his free hand. "They're about."

"I haven't seen Aften at all tonight—he okay?"

"Why does everyone keep asking about him?"

"Dude I just hadn't seen him."

Matthew sloshed in place. "My car has been stolen but sure let's wonder where Aften is."

"Matt, fuck off." Mercer found himself getting angry too frequently and paused to slow his breathing. "I mean...we just worry."

"Then why was he invited?"

"It was either he be here or alone."

Both stopped, knowing well that neither was a healthy option.

Matthew interrupted the silence. "I shouldn't have come."

"No, no, you—"

"Don't try...try to argue with that. I could've stayed at home. Hell, maybe then the van wouldn't have been stolen either." He punctuated his speculation with a forced laugh.

There was another awkward pause before Matthew continued: "I'm pretty sure—I mean, I *know*—Aften isn't okay. He was acting really odd before we left. I knew as much when he came out in Ethan's hoodie—"

"—I noticed that—"

"—but I didn't want to ask about it."

Matthew had no idea how to broach the topic of the obscene amounts of blood, and opted instead not to. That not only wouldn't help, but would cement him as being an asshole and he wasn't inclined to face that reality in the moment. "Another shot?"

They both drank.

Beyond the kitchen window Matthew and Mercer watched Heather's van pull slowly, uncomfortably into the gravel. August stepped out and with much more haste proceeded indoors, hanging the keys back on the doorside hook. August locked eyes briefly with Matthew—both of whom said nothing for both knew the situation was unacceptable—before disappearing into the living room. Mercer looked stunned and was in the process of asking what the fuck had happened before Matthew cut him off. "He can't un-steal the car. What good would it do to address it now?"

Mercer, in the kindest way possible, said to Matthew, "You are absolutely useless."

August was texting furiously.
Belfry we need to leave
hello?
Belfry!!!

Belfry picked up her phone, frustrated at August's persistent messages.

what? Where are you?

I just got back

but where

I cant tell you we just need to leave

**hey I can't drive right now
and you shouldn't be either**

the police are on the way

**huh??
why?
what did you do?**

look I just got fucked okay, get your keys

Ethan raked his nails up the side of Aften's ribs before withdrawing and reconnecting with a forceful punch, and another, and another while driving his cock deep into Aften, who moaned with each thrust and strike. Aften's eyes were watering in rapturous torment, small trails running down cheeks and wetting Ethan's hand as it knocked into Aften's jaw. Another blow. Another blow. This time to the neck. This time to the eye. A slow pressure released and with his tongue, Aften began collecting the stream of blood seeping from his nose. Small claws prodded his cheeks and tested the blood with their own tiny, sinister tongues and Aften thrashed until the curious, insidious creatures scattered.

  He watched Ethan's eyes with intent, beady black nothings seen only as the slightest of glints. An arm stretched forward, flinching instinctively with each punch to the side—Aften tightened his fingers slowly, teasingly around Ethan's neck and with a sudden force and fervor pulled Ethan's head down, slamming their foreheads together, grins mirroring the other's.

Aften wrapped his legs behind Ethan, his grip growing stronger as Ethan's drool fell to his face. Each part of his body was of devilish heat, bound by welcome anger and lascivious movement to scrape and scream with each ream and faked apology. Nails dug into backs, through skin, through fire, and along Aften's arms crawled the small, dainty bodies of his creation, waiting for the chance to sink teeth into regret. Ethan grabbed the side of Aften's torso with such force it felt almost as if something had ruptured.

A laugh gurgled below a choke, a laugh of intent, a pressured declaration, a whisper to Ethan and to God and all the demons within and without that Ethan was not going to leave this room.

Aften dug his teeth in Ethan's neck—Ethan, his nails into hips—Aften's legs constricted further—Ethan's began to thrash and pound and writhe—a limitless swarm fell atop and crawled below and scattered around them, picking skin, clawing feet, tugging hair, gnawing meat, ravaging Ethan from ego to flesh to bone.

"Aften, that's—" Elation turned to fear.

Another bite, another gasp, another much more forceful punch as Ethan's thrusting grew harder, tenser, violent even. Nails that previously scratched felt soft as skin collected beneath them, pillowing each scrape. Salt tickled his tongue while he pulled free from Ethan's darkening neck and threw his head back, just as a flailing wrist slammed into Aften's esophagus. Silence followed, blood rushed, room spun, and Ethan howled as he pulled free of Aften who now possessed a chunk of Ethan's neck between his teeth. Ethan tumbled to the floor, and a mound of crawling, hungry phantoms soon surrounded him, smothering him, muffling yelps and cries between hardwood and fur as thrashing turned to twitching turned to nothing at all. Aften swallowed heavily.

After much sweating and silence, Aften slowly raised himself upward, arms strained, back aching, the room, the world quieter. His eyes strained to see much as his legs strained to stand, and as his cock grew soft and his body weary, acrid realization washed over him with a soft *kick* into a limp figure sprawled on the floor.

[unintelligible]
      [*bang!*]
           [unintelligible]

Belfry raised an eyebrow and looked up from her phone, just as she watched Jessíka turn the corner and begin up the stairs.

Even with music resonating among the partygoers, Sara and Heather were strikingly loud. Much of the room had grown quiet and apprehensive in response, an air of discomfort growing prevalent among the house's onlookers. No sooner had August entered the room did the two aggress, Heather demanding answers, Sara demanding he leave. "Okay, okay, fine—I'm leaving," he said, holding his palms up in surrender, "I just—"

"You just nothing," Sara interrupted, surprisingly composed. August's quick agreement calmed her, so long as he left. Beer and liquor grew still in people's hands, eyes grew equally still locked on the three of them. Heather took notice, calming her voice and brushing her hair aside in a confused uncertainty of how to respond next. Yet, a series of lights soon alleviated her of that responsibility. "Shit, *shit!*"

Many heads turned, and whether it were the drugs, the noise, or the general fear of police, chaos broke out in the living room as people scattered to collect their keys, their friends, their booze, quickly abandon said booze, and dispersed from the house like inebriated cockroaches. August abandoned the group to search for Belfry (who had sooner abandoned the group (again)). Sara began making an effort to stow away the pipes littering the coffee table as Heather vanished into another room to find Matthew. Mercer, with the placidity of one who had done nothing wrong, merely turned off his music. Sara's house remained an orchestra of loud muttering and footsteps.

"Why are they here?"

"Did we do something wrong?"

"None of this is—well, *most* of this isn't illegal."

Knock, knock.

Silence.

"...well...Sara, get the door."

Sara appeared shocked at such commanding impertinence.

"Hey, it's your house."

Again, knocking, though this time more heavily driving into the wood.

Sara scoffed before approaching the door, straightening her hair, and opening her home to the police officer standing on her porch. "Can I help you?"

"Hello," the officer said with obligatory kindness. She clearly did not wish to be out at one o'clock, such was clear on her face. "We received a noise complaint?"

"Okay," Sara answered swiftly. "We'll turn the music down. Anything else?"

The officer laughed lightly under her breath. She did not answer. Rather, she turned her head to the side. Sara followed her gaze, seeing first the stream of a flashlight, then a person, turn the corner of her property.

"Well?" The officer at the door asked her partner.

The second officer stepped to the entryway. "Ma'am—" oh, how Sara disliked that— "I'm Officer Lewis. This," he motioned towards his partner, "is Officer Page. We received several noise complaints—"

"I've been told," Sara interrupted.

"—and were coming by to address such, but..."

Officer Lewis licked his teeth. Sara remained quiet, as did everyone listening in the room behind her.

"...I couldn't help but notice while walking up here that two particular cars are in your driveway. We'd like to ask you a few questions."

Her footsteps felt heavy with each laborious motion, the night growing more and more a weight upon her back. Jessíka ascended the steps. Mercer's words circled within her; they spoke themselves over and over until the concept of processing them was foreign. They simply were.

She stared forward, paying little attention to the cocktail of voices, ignoring how she nearly tripped on the final step, and only briefly glancing at the fractured wood framing Mercer's doorknob. Perhaps she had simply never noticed, she reasoned. Such was irrelevant—she needed his coat.

Jessíka opened the door in what was the longest second to exist, and a dim hallway light begat a shocked and naked Aften, beneath whom was the ravaged body of both her and his former lover. Blood pooled beneath it, filling in the rivers between floorboards and tasting the feet of the bed, Aften's feet just barely above the liquid themselves. Jessíka locked eyes with him and could lend tangibility to his paralysis in the depths of her being, the delicate balance of shock and knowing, each of them equal parts of the same scale.

Jessíka stepped forward—Aften leaned back, a stifled sob attempted to free itself—and then she let Mercer's door shut softly behind her before again locking eyes with the darkened outline of Aften. It was amazing, Jessíka pondered, how so many thoughts at one time felt like she wasn't able to think at all. *What...happened here?*

"Put your pants on."

Aften hastily did as he was told. "I..."

She waved her hand, either silencing or ignoring him—in either case, she did not hear anything else he had to say. No excuses. *I don't need any excuses, not really. He's dead. Ethan is dead.* A glance to the side. *Saphi is dead. Aften may as well be. What excuse could undo any of this?*

Aften sat in silence broken only by his quivering as a shadowed Jessíka stood above him. He prepared for a scream, for a cry, for Jessíka to escape down the stairs and evacuate the home. He was not prepared for what happened instead.

"Aften, do you trust me?"

While his expression was hidden, his movement was clear—he was surprised, Jessíka knew. When he did not answer, she repeated herself. "I asked, 'Do you trust me?'"

There was a long silence as blood painted Jessíka's soles, but this silence was eventually followed by Aften's questioning intonation: "...n-no?"

"Well, I need you to." Jessíka stepped forward again; Aften jolted less forcefully this time, though still visibly. She could hear the gulped cries and the swallowed spit. He was scared, she knew. Jessíka pulled her shoes off and gently laid them beneath the bedframe before—one knee at a time—crawling onto the bed beside her murderous friend.

"I don't understand."

"Turn around."

Aften did so with reluctance. He was in no position to argue. By the time he had, Jessíka had already flipped open her pocket knife, which Aften noticed—too late—as she grabbed him by the wrist. He opened his mouth, eyes wet, their whites showing clear, even in such a bleak night, yet Jessíka remained still and waited patiently. She knew he wouldn't scream. What good would it do? And she knew that *Aften* knew the same thing.

Knife still in hand, she placed her hand to his wrist and gently traced the outline of his forearm until— "Ah, there it is." —she had located the fabric of his suicide attempt not hours before. Aften was still as stone save for the occasional shudder. Chirps and hums leaked from the night air through the windows and decorated their mutual uncertainty with the sound of insects.

Jessíka turned his arm about and dragged the blade down the length of it, deep red welling against the dim skin.

Aften went to pull back only to find Jessíka's grip stronger than he expected.

"Shut up." Again, she pulled the darkened silver against his flesh.

He let out a soft moan, tears forming in the corners of his eyes—he wrapped his free hand around Jessíka's wrist, his blood leaking onto her knees, a macabre arrhythmic patter.

"It needs to look like a struggle."

"What?"

"If you leave here with no injuries, it will be obvious you murdered him." She tapped the inside of his wrist with the pocket knife; he winced. "But if you have knife wounds, then you can claim he assaulted you first. It wouldn't be the first time, would it?"

No verbal answer was provided. Instead, Aften simply released her wrist. Jessíka, however, did not return the favor. "Good boy." This time, his other arm.

Soon, between cries and gasps, Aften's arms were decorated with mock shows of battle, of struggle, Jessíka maintaining both clear expression and movement for the entire duration. She knew it hurt, and in truth she wished it didn't—she had no intention of acting as a judge of Aften's actions. What good would his hurt do for her anyway? She needed his trust, not his pain. Her fingers grew strained in such a tight grip around both wrist and knife, but with no more opposition and unhealthy desensitization, she was able to complete her grisly work. Aften was sobbing mutely when she finally released his arm. The bedsheets could be felt staining. She aimlessly smeared the blood between her forefinger and thumb. Everything had become eerily quiet.

"Now, I need a favor from you."

"Again, may we come in?"

"Again, no."

This time, the answer was not quite so satisfactory, and Officer Page's boot connected with the door, flinging it past Sara with a *slam!* into the wall perpendicular. Sara's at-ease demeanor was at conflict with her rapidly beating heart. Officer Page stepped in, followed silently by Officer Lewis. "Sure smells like someone shouldn't argue with us in here."

As expected, no one argued. All present knew well such would be a losing battle, whether or not they were granted permission. Sara turned and glared at August, who turned away in evident guilt. Sara clenched her fists. Belfry appeared from behind the kitchen doorframe upon hearing the loud *bang,* then paused in her tracks and stared at the floor. Officer Lewis regarded her with curiosity before passively dismissing her. It was Heather that spoke. "Hello, forgive the mess. Obviously you guys are here for a reason, what can we do to make this as easy as possible for you?"

"You can tell us who owns the blue van out back."

Heather gulped. "Uh," she turned around to the rest of the room. "Anyone...know whose van that is?"

Everyone—almost unanimously—knowing it to be Heather's looked to the police:

"Not sure."

"No idea."

"Sorry—I don't."

Page and Lewis looked at each other in knowing disapproval. Officer Lewis excused himself to make a phone call, at which Officer Page nodded before speaking, directing her eyes towards August. "Let's make something clear: I know you're withholding the truth. Now either you can all go to jail for obvious drug paraphernalia, or *one* of you can. We know the car to be registered to one Heather Torres; where is she?"

Sara broke the silence. "She's Heather."

"Oh *fuck* you Sara!"

"I'm not getting dragged into anything because you decided to break the law."

"Oh, okay, that's rich coming from the one with booze and cocaine in every inch of this house."

"Cocaine?" Sara sounded sincerely surprised.

"Are you kidding me?"

"Hey, hey!" Officer Page threw her hands up and stepped between the two women. She turned to Heather. "And where is the man that was driving your car during the time of the wreck?"

"I don't know what you're talking about, it was just—"

"It was her boyfriend Matt."

"Belfry are you serious!"

"Hey, I'm on Sara's side here."

"Oh, we're taking *sides* now?"

"Wait, Belfry?" Officer Lewis interjected.

At that moment, Belfry's phone began to ring, with Officer Lewis approaching as she fumbled to silence it. "Belfry. You're that girl from the liquor store earlier."

Belfry stammered at such recognition.

Officer Lewis cancelled his call, at which point so too did Belfry's phone stop ringing. "You're at a party on the same day of a robbery, with a Mustang just as seen on your store's surveillance just a few hours ago?"

Belfry's face grew red beneath her similarly red hair. "I assure you, I didn't see the car that left the store earlier, I sw—"

"It's her brother's car! His name is August."

"Fuck *off* Heather!"

Officer Page turned towards the accused. "August, is this true?"

The arguing in the room ceased, and even for all its manifest anger and outrage, one consensus could be reached. "August," Sara said softly. "How did Officer Page know you were the one we were talking about?"

More lights began flashing in the periphery of Sara's windows.

Aften was both shivering and crying. His arms ached and his face stung with tears, which fell and mixed with blood atop the sheets. His skin was testament to agony, his eyes to fear; everything around him felt as though it belonged in fiction, that there was simply no way his life fell to this in mere hours. People were yelling downstairs, yet despite this, Jessíka seemed unphased—she did not quake, she did not cry—her vague features seemed simply to rest upon an otherwise blank palette.

She held his hand—softer than before—and rubbed her thumb into the grooves of his palms. There was an unexpected, unfamiliar kindness to the motion, a mixture of both ache and welcome that confused him. Aften found himself with tears rolling down his cheeks, thoughts running through his head—meaningless apologies, unretractable actions—oh, how had he ruined himself.

Lightly, Jessíka pushed the hilt of the pocket knife into his hand, fingers tracing fingers, metal growing damp, and through the blur Aften stared down at the tainted blade. "Aften," Jessíka said, "I need you to kill me."

"I...what?" Aften was taken aback. Jessíka's demeanor—her straightforwardness, her emotionless request—felt unreal, as though she were already dead and simply looking for closure. Aften shook his head. "No, n-no; I—" he punctuated each word with throat-wrenching gasp, swallow, gasp. "You can't...can't ask me to do that."

"Oh, I can." Jessíka wasted no time with such a response.

"What, I—" Aften stammered, lost. "What about Sara?"

That hurt. *Fuck*. Jessíka didn't have an answer. That was the worst part.

She curled Aften's fingers around the knife's shank before pulling it up, higher, until it was gracing the base of her jaw. She ignored the question. *How could I possibly answer it?* For all her love toward Sara, the burden of the world, of being, weighed upon her relentlessly. It wasn't that she didn't love, or even that she thought she wasn't loved herself—it was the endless battle raging within her, and she was tired of being a perpetual casualty. "I'm scared, Aften. How'd you do it?"

"What?"

"How'd you become strong enough to try?"

Aften was at a loss for words. Strength? Is that what that was? "I can't—"

"You *will*." An uncharacteristic aggression pushed forth from Jessíka. There was fire in her voice and the ability to will in her tone. "If I'm dead, it will look like Ethan killed me. You'll have stumbled upon the scene and defended yourself."

"Why...why can't I have saved you, why do you need to be *dead*."

"Because I *want* to be dead, Aften." It was uncomfortable to him, how Jessíka did not cry. Aften could hardly stomach it. Ethan's body watched the ceiling, soaking, unknowing. Jessíka pressed Aften's hand harder against her neck. "Either you kill me, or you go to jail. I'm your last witness."

"Is that a threat?"

"If it needs to be."

Soft splashes sounded as blood trickled from the edge of the bed and onto the floor below. Bugs seemed to grow quieter, a somber respect for the dead, the dying. Beneath them, flashing lights began to grow present, and while distant, while cornered beyond their room, the slightest light managed to circle its way into the otherwise sepulchral chamber. It was in that moment Aften saw the genuinity plastered across Jessíka's features—the pleading formed in the edges of her quivering lips, the way her hand struggled not to shiver below her jawline, the despondency pooled in the whites of her eyes.

Aften began sobbing—his head was light—his throat corrosive—every part of him felt as though it were both burning and glacial at once, a monument to irony, a monument to self-pity. It was here that Jessíka's expression began to waver and her stoicism gave way to tears. Coughing between staggered breaths, shuddering heavier, she and Aften shared a grasp of one another. Soon they were in movement, both gasping, both exhaling, both miserable and useless and the others' salvation all in a single room, two separate bodies with the shared goal of needing one of them dead. Aften pushed, and pushed, and pushed the knife further, deeper into Jessíka's skin, too afraid to pull either direction, too afraid to close the curtains on the life of his friend whom he needed, whom Sara needed, whom she herself deserved to need too—he was sweating—she was crying—both knew what needed to happen—both were terrified—and Jessíka—sad, kind Jessíka—gripped

Aften's hand in an unearthly tightness, twisted her head with one final inhale, and allowed the knife to perform its grisly task.

Aften began shaking as blood spouted before him. Jessíka fell back, gurgling, breathing breaths that no longer mattered into a world that no longer mattered. Aften pushed himself back and stumbled from the side of the bed, careful to avoid the blood, kicking himself back into a corner staring at the room, the three bodies—Jessíka, Saphi, Ethan—looking towards each other, towards everything, towards nothing all at once, a tripartite of regret, of necessity, of fear and defense and confusion.

The knife in his hand was inexplicably warm, fiery, seeping from his fingertips to his tendons to the multiplicity of hells and selves clawing into the world around him. He tossed the knife next to Ethan; it spun in the puddle of blood beside the body, coating it in saturnine sanguine, alleviating it of one sin and decorating it with another.

Aften buried his face in his hands until Jessíka's moaning ceased and her head tilted to the side, mouth agape, throat agape. After a year of silence, of guttural choking, of desecration of body, home, and friendships, he knew what he needed to do. Aften slowly—struggling, aching—leaned his head back, clutched one arm across the other as he pulled his knees up, and screamed with what voice remained and strained and agonized "Help!" into the winter.

Mercer and Sara stood to the wall adjacent to the remainder of the living room, filled more now with officers than friends.

 August—armed robbery;
 Belfry—accomplice to armed robbery;
 Matthew—fleeing the scene of a crime;

and Heather—similarly fleeing the scene of a crime.

The latter two silently opted not to incriminate Aften in their wreck.

Many words were being said though very few were being heard, and it was not until Sara's four friends—hereby a tentative title—had been escorted from her home did a hellish shriek from above them command attention. It was Page that first ascended the stairs, demanding to know "Who else is here!" yet the question went unanswered as Sara squeezed past and flung herself through the first available door—

"Oh...oh my g—no, no, no, n-no, no..." Speech fell to muttering to wailing to a slow walk forward as the flashlight halo behind her illuminated the grotesque scene before her. Indistinct radio chatter sounded behind her, alongside spectral *"ma'am"*'s and *"—can't"*'s that Sara pushed aside. Her beautiful Jessíka was sprawled about, a mock crucifixion; the headboard stared down upon her, upon Sara, upon the floor-bound Ethan. Her fists grew so tight that nails drew purple trenches into her palm and her teeth clenched so that sound was replaced by clouded throbbing.

Sara then began to scream and then, in what shocked the room still, began to viciously, mercilessly stomp Ethan's corpse, and for all the discussion and yelling and ringing in ears, somehow the distinct, soft squelching of Ethan's body below such force rose above it all.

The otherwise still Aften began lightly rocking in the corner, his head in his hands, until even behind shut eyes the presence of light was clear. An unfamiliar voice questioned him, demanding to know what happened, asking "who" and "what" and "how" questions that Aften could not wholly discern. He looked up, and behind the meaningless officer he watched Sara being pulled nails-from-doorframe, screaming, shouting as if any known decibel could will Jessíka back. *Thank you, Sara,* he thought, stifling the slightest of smirks. *Desecrating the body like that,* well...it muddies my involvement. Jessíka was right. It just needs to look like defense.

As all before them, the police attempted the lightswitch just to realize it would not work, then Lewis clamored in, demanding answers, before the scene of Aften became apparent and an air of comfort instead washed over him, "Hey, hey, let's get you downstairs."

And so—sobbing, *as one should*, he thought—downstairs Aften went.

The questions were uncomfortably simple. The more Aften answered, the easier he found it to continue.

"I went upstairs for some time alone from the party." His injuries had since been bandaged. The cuts were bleeding, but due to Jessíka's thoughtful precision, they were neither deep nor fatal. Part of Aften regretted that—the other part wanted to see what would come next.

Sara was being comforted (ineffectively) at the kitchen counter as more authorities began to arrive, making a display of their treks up, down, up, down the stairs again as they obtained whatever information they were pursuing.

"I don't know why Ethan killed her, I...I thought they were friends."

Occasionally the police came downstairs with objects in tiny little bags, the first Aften noticed being the pocket knife. Everyone's chatter made it difficult to focus on the questions asked. "Uhm...could—could you repeat the question?" and so the officer did.

"Wait, cat?" Aften asked. "He killed Saphi too?"

Sara screamed from the other room, evidently hearing this declaration. Her sentences were falling apart at the seams, pooling into words and emotion that constructed no communication, but presented their emotion well enough—she was absolutely, irrevocably heartbroken.

"No, I didn't know that part, I..." Aften rubbed his nose and cleared his throat, massaging his burning eyes. "I don't know what happened. I came upstairs and Ethan had already killed her. He tried for me next, and..."

Mercer rubbed Aften's back as he began blubbering through his fingers, tears pouring through the cracks in his hands and painting the carpet with sorrow. "I'm so sorry, I'm so sorry, I wasn't—I wasn't fast enough." A now-swollen eye pulsed angrily with each heave. *Excellent*.

Officer Page seemed an expert at maintaining emotional distance; thankfully, Mercer was not so skilled. "Aften you cannot blame yourself, we should have known this would happen."

Page raised her eyebrow. "Had...Ethan shown signs of aggression in the past?"

"Oh, oh yes," Mercer responded immediately. He similarly cleared a cry threatening to surface. "Ethan's had bursts in the past, but nothing this...this serious—"

Perfect. "This serious?" Aften feigned anger, his voice rising, his hands shaking. "Ethan broke my arm! My wrist was shattered in two places!"

Saying Ethan's name like this, over and over—*Ethan, Ethan*—served as a sickening catharsis, a passing of blame, an alleviation of guilt Aften deserved not to be rid of, and yet—

"You're right Aften, I'm sorry, I shouldn't have chosen that word."

There was a respite in questions, though not in noise. Footsteps still echoed from the stairs, and while Sara's crying had grown quieter it was still evident. For all its bodies, the house felt so staggeringly lonely.

"So...Aften," Officer Page started again, "Tell me of the events one more time."

It was in the best interest of everyone that they be removed from the house as quickly as possible. Officer Page had since left, while Officer Lewis offered to stay until everyone was comfortably relocated. Sara's house was no longer in position to house people. An ambulance was illuminating the night on Sara's front lawn. While the officers present insisted Aften be taken to the hospital, he vehemently refused, stating he *would* go the hospital but *would not* pay for the ambulance.

Of course, Aften had no intention of going to the hospital. Paying for that was similarly out of the question. His arms and head and heart ached but not enough to warrant a price tag. He would be satisfied with a shower.

Sara assured everyone (unconvincingly) that she would be fine as she waited for her mother to arrive. Aften could not bring himself to say anything to her beyond platitudes. He felt bad for her, or for himself; he had a difficult time identifying which. Sara, Mercer, and Aften hugged for what felt like a warm, morose century before Mercer grabbed his keys, insistent on delivering Aften safely home.

"Where is Matt and Heather?"

"We'll talk about that tomorrow." Mercer quickly silenced him.

And so, with the promise that the police would remain in touch, Aften and Mercer carefully, quietly and downtrodden crawled into Mercer's car and began their vanishment into the crepuscule air of 4 a.m..

Streetlights existed in bizarre limbo, some remaining on, others flickering with movement, some already acknowledging the brightening horizon. They drove past familiar roads, familiar trees, a familiar church—

"It will stay green."

"Thanks."

Conversation was scarce. Mercer seemed cold; the police wouldn't let him retrieve a coat before they left. For all the weight and sorrow and horror, the car felt empty, both in its people and its emotion, as if two spirits were existing beside one another, incapable of traversing planes to discuss their uniform death. A combined-though-separate fugue state of being(s).

"We will make this one too." They skated by just as it shifted from yellow to red.

"That was a close one."

Aften did not respond.

Trucks were beginning to awaken, their corporate pilgrimages set to resume. Metal goliaths occasionally crossed their paths, though this far from the interstate they were few and far between. The roads were narrow and lonesome, the trees the usual company. Another light was soon ahead, Aften's home not far thereafter. A subtle memory of but ten hours old tickled his mind, a simple phrase that conceived his night.

"Well?"

Aften played with his hands and stared at his feet. The floor mats were surprisingly clean. He couldn't help but notice the light scratches on the underside of the dashboard, remnants of transport, of boots laid atop it, of travel, of friends. He wondered if Sara's trip was as quiet and austere as theirs was. He wondered when Heather and Matthew were going to arrive home. He knew that ultimately he would never get away with the evening, and with such truth felt a twinge of regret that Mercer was to become a part of his solution.

Closer they grew to the stoplight ahead, and again Mercer asked for direction. Aften picked at his bloodied knuckles, rubbed his tattered arms, watched as tiny hands crept their way from below the cushion, then said with quiet decisiveness. "Keep going. It'll be fine."

Aften was lying, and a small smile played with the corner of his lips as he did so. The red light before them remained locked in its ominous glow and as Mercer drove, trust placed in Aften, a truck plunged through the intersection. Aften felt the impact, the impacts of the evening; Mercer too. Glass shattered, metal crumpled, and horns blared as Mercer's little sedan flipped and scraped against the asphalt. Aften's head spun, his arms grew weak, and as Mercer's voice faded away, Aften's breathing settled into a paced—though shallow—resignation—and he could not help but think, but reflect, how strange it was that the world crashing down around him could be so quiet.

Late afternoon sunlight crept through windows, blinds draped carpet, and as a soft *click* signaled the arrival of people, Biscuit darted from the bed and meekly *meowww*ed at the two familiar figures entering his home.

Heather and Matthew—tired and frustrated—stepped into the apartment as Matthew's cat danced dangerously with their footsteps. They had been gone the better part of two days, the first for their involvement in hitting a car the night before, and the second for questioning regarding knowledge of Ethan's death. They had no answers for their interrogators, which while seemingly not believed did not offer enough reason to keep them. They were given a court date and a very clear declaration that the police would be contacting them with additional questions. Such felt more as a threat.

They had not heard from Sara (which they expected), but not from Aften or Mercer either (which they did not expect). It was easy to assume August and Belfry were similarly at the mercy of the police. In any case, Matthew was not inclined to worry for them, not after Belfry let the officers know they were responsible for the drive. Had it not been for her, they may have been able to talk through it (or at least, that's what he justified to himself).

Biscuit interrupted their aggravated musing with another accusatory *Meow!* of abandonment, and Heather led him to the kitchen to be fed. His two bowls were bone-dry.

In the sink sat a dirtied mug, aged coffee having coagulated at its base. She thought of Aften. *How did he manage to survive? What happened between Ethan and Jessíka?* It was too much to process in such a small window, and for each question asked her head swam with a headache as she attempted to find reason.

And then came the guilt.

I should have been there, Matthew thought, recalling the sheer terror on his friend's face as the police shuffled him down those horrendously narrow stairs. *What will Sara do?* he continued, fearing for her emotional state— Jessíka had been her whole world. He wanted to check in on her, but between a dead phone and only one call available to them while held for questioning, Matthew hadn't had the chance. At least, that's what he told himself. In the deepest recesses of his mind, he wondered how likely he was to actually contact anyone involved. The night was awful—it was a horrific event that preceded now horrific memories and Matthew couldn't help but wonder how different things would have been if only…if only any of them had been willing to challenge the precarious balance that held their relations to one another together.

Matthew pushed his forehead to the wall. Never had eggshell white drywall been so comforting. *I should have stayed home. We should have stayed home.* He looked to the side, seeing the soft specks of red in the carpet, against the doorframe of the hallway bathroom.

And then too late came the rage.

Heather slammed a palm to the countertop, causing a startled Biscuit to bristle and gaze up just in time to see Heather begin to cry. It was a soft, angry cry—a cry she didn't want, a cry that felt like Sara's and Ethan's and August's and Beltry's fault for the *sheer fucking stupidity* of even hosting a party with such a group in the first place. Hindsight plagued her. She realized too how it was equal parts her passivity in inviting Aften. *But...after all, Aften did kill Ethan right? In self-defense of course after seeing Jessika but... what if he hadn't been there?* Heather couldn't put her thoughts together. The entire night felt unreal. Just thinking the word "kill" made her want to vomit. A pause, a breath—Heather realized then that for all her fury and disgust, for all the guilt in bringing Aften, she wondered who Ethan may have killed next had it not been for him.

Then, with a strange shared lucidity, Heather and Matthew—despite their own exhaustion—realized Aften should have been home by now. They knew at the very least that he likely left with Mercer—and yet, after a night of everything going wrong, recognizing they should have come home to their roommate, the two could not face processing something else having happened, something else going wrong.

The evening settled over the building in a cold silence as yet another night began to approach. The previous softness of the setting sun now felt abrasive. Frost ravaged leaves, wind berated the building—unforgiving bitterness persisted, and darkness slowly engulfed the night. For all the bugs still sang their nightly elegies, for all the clouds still moved, for all the trees still swayed, for all these souls remained hollow—everything was the same. Everything had to be the same. And if everything were the same, then surely—*surely*—everything must be fine.

other titles from Sinister Stoat Press

The Last Book You'll Ever Read by Scott Hughes
The Saint of Witches by Avra Margariti
Bone by Aaron J. Muller
Cause for Concern by Neil S. Reddy
The Devil had a Black Dog by Jonathan W. Thurston
Spiders in our Bed by Jonathan W. Thurston
Body & Blood edited by Weasel
Carnage by Weasel
Dread edited by Weasel
The Haunted Traveler edited by Weasel
Incendiary edited by Weasel
Ghostly Pornographers by Thomas White

www.ingramcontent.com/pod-product-compliance
Lightning Source LLC
Chambersburg PA
CBHW021320110426
42743CB00050B/3430